LEADER
of the
BAND

ALSO BY SCOTT LANG

Leadership Success DVD/CD-Rom
Leadership Travel Guide
Leadership Travel Guide Workbook
Leadership Survival Guide DVD/CD-Rom

LEADER
of the
BAND

Lessons for the Young
Teacher in All of Us

Scott Lang

GIA Publications
CHICAGO

Leader of the Band
Scott Lang

GIA Publications, Inc.
7404 S Mason Ave
Chicago IL 60638

www.giamusic.com

Copyright © 2011 GIA Publications, Inc.
All rights reserved.
Printed in the United States of America.

Cover and author photos courtesy Nellie Welter.

G-8053
ISBN: 978-1-57999-848-6

To Julie Duty, my long ago student, former colleague and current friend. Thank you for being smart enough to know when I was wrong, strong enough to tell me, wise enough to know how, and caring enough to know when. This book would not be what it is without you. Through this process, you have proven, once again, to be a great teacher.

P.S. I would like the 1st Alto part to "Hounds of Spring" back, please.

To my mother, Sheila Donatelle. If this book were about extraordinary mothers, yours would be the first and only chapter.

Contents

INTRODUCTION 3

1 BOBBY KNIGHT AND ME 11
   On humility with Richard Saucedo of Carmel High School

2 MAC VS PC AND THE ATTACK OF THE KILLER TOMATOES 39
   On finding your fit with David Duarté of the Deer Valley Unified School District

3 SAMMY THE BULL 67
   On creating a culture with Darrin Davis of Broken Arrow High School

4 A PE-KING DUCK OUT OF WATER 97
   On connecting with your community with Michael Boitz of Saratoga High School

5 SIX DEGREES FROM KEVIN BACON 129
   On connecting with peers with Dr. Nola Jones of the University of Tennessee Martin

6 LEONARDO DA VINCI AND THE CHOCOLATE CHIP COOKIE 155
   On being a professional with Scott Rush of Wando High School

7 THE DYNAMICS OF LIFE 192
   On maintaining perspective with Diana Williams of Webb City High School

8 GLORIA STEINEM PASSES THE BATON 221
   On dealing with change with Jo Ann Hood of John Overton High School

9 JUMPING OFF THE LADDER 250
   On professional status in music education with Terry Jolley of Siegel Middle School

ABOUT THE AUTHOR 277

LEADER
of the
BAND

Introduction

Almost all of us have the guilty pleasure of a "bathroom bookshelf." You know what I'm talking about. Simple-minded material designed to captivate, cultivate, and entertain our minds when there is little else to do. It might be a newspaper, magazine, catalogue, trivia book, or something more substantial, but nonetheless, there it sits, patiently waiting for your return. It does not take the place of your more academic works. It knows its place in the world. Honestly, it doesn't take a work of genius to garner the attention of someone whose only contemplative thoughts center around "paper up, or down?" and "two ply, or four?" While men typically use these masterpieces of brevity more than women, I would be remiss if I did not mention that in our eight-square-foot library, my wife keeps the latest copy of *O Magazine*. It would also be a lie if I didn't admit to thumbing through it myself on occasion.

These quiet-time tomes understand their niche and fill a need, albeit not an important one. The concept of bathroom reading has been around for as long as indoor plumbing, and although I am not able to lay my hands on any empirical data, I suspect this has been a daily ritual in some way, shape, or form since we developed the outhouse. Ah yes. The outhouse. Now *that* was an important invention. Not only did it allow for a sense of privacy and convenience, it stopped us from having to worry about being eaten by something while we were finishing our "business." Think about it. Where once man had to be hyper-vigilant and uber-aware as he stood or sat, exposed to people and predators alike, now we sit with nothing else to do, alone with our thoughts.

This book is not designed to be a bathroom reader. It is, however, designed to be a "prep hour" reader. The thoughts, ideas, and stories contained within are intended to be consumed in short bursts of time and be easily digestible. I hope that you feel as if you are actively involved in the dialogue with the individuals presented here. Feel free to shout out a question from time to time; just make sure your building administrator isn't within earshot. Your students... well, they are probably used to you muttering things out loud. They won't even give it a second thought.

For those who see our modern day, 24/7/365, ultra-connected, constantly multitasking world as something new, I point you to the bathroom reader as proof positive that as a civilization, we have been multitasking for centuries. We have been using these trips to the bathroom for more than Mother Nature intended since the beginning. If you find this discussion a little uncomfortable, if not puerile, I point to Rodin's great sculpture, *The Thinker* as proof that great minds not only think alike, but do it in the same place. Sure, I can't prove that is what he is doing, but I have never seen that pose from someone doing anything but that. *The Thinker* just might be our first indicator that multitasking existed long before technology.

Music teachers are masters of multitasking. We can attend a staff meeting, chart a halftime show, listen to publishers' CDs, and text our spouses, all while secretly playing with the Facebook feature on our new smartphone. The only time band directors are not doing three things at once is when we are teaching, and even then, our minds are racing with a thousand thoughts as we work to keep pace with the hundreds of notes being played each and every second. When standing on the podium, we are in the *Zone*, wholly consumed, focused, and in the moment. We are human supercomputers, processing thousands of bytes of information through our MIDI ports (ears) and into our mainframes (minds). This is what we do best and why we put up with all of the rest. It is our time of Zen and place of purpose. For these too-few moments, we endure the rest of our day. In this special place, we take refuge from the outside world, step away from the distractions, and live in the present moment.

* * *

By nature, we remember the bad more clearly than the good. We remember 9/11 with greater clarity than 9/10. We remember the horror of John F. Kennedy's assassination more than the hopes and dreams associated with his administration. As music educators, we are no different. We remember the few wrong notes during a performance more than the thousands played correctly. We remember the flaws of the performance rather than the successes. We remember the tunes that crashed and burned, rather than the phrases that soared over the audience. We remember the heartbreaking performances more than the life affirming ones. These difficult moments are not displayed in a trophy cabinet or relived at the end-of-the-year banquet, but they are the moments we remember nonetheless. Having said that, as you read through these pages, I want you to actively look for the qualities that you share with these educators as hard as you look for what separates you. I know this goes against your nature as a perfectionist and educator, but work with me on this.

My hope is that the stories of these nine directors will both educate and inspire you. I want you to see not just the differences between you and them, but the similarities as well. I want you to celebrate as much as you commiserate and to reflect on where you have achieved success and where you have failed to rise to what is possible. No one person contains all the character traits of great teaching, which is why it took nine different individuals to tell this story. So, as you read, go easy on yourself and be realistic about not only who you are, but who they are as well. Oh yeah... and turn off the ten o'clock news and curl up with this book, as we should all spend more time with people we admire. I encourage you to read this book in small doses. Read a little, think a little, and dream a little. If you were able to spend time with the people mentioned in the book one on one, wouldn't you want to savor the experience and extend it for as long as possible? Well, consider this book your personal conversation with some wonderful people. If you allow these people into your life the way they have allowed me into their lives, you just might see some of yourself in them.

As is the case with my other leadership offerings, this book is not designed to give you The Answer. I don't believe there is one answer to any problem. To that end, I do not think there is any one way to teach music. You may even find contradictory beliefs contained within this book. My goal in shining a light on these very special individuals is to share the stories of my friends and colleagues who have achieved success in some very laudable ways and share my thoughts on some values that I think are worthy of your consideration. They are people who have inspired me, and they serve as the embodiment of the belief that with hope, hard work, vision, and commitment, all things are possible. In these people, I have found that greatness is not something to be displayed, but something to be discussed.

The teachers whose stories are captured within these pages are not alone in their attainment of excellence. When I thought about writing this book, a flood of names came to mind. Probably the same names that come to your mind. These are the iconic names of people who have helped to shape the lives of students and our entire profession. There was only one problem: I didn't know them. Sure, I may have met them, seen them conduct, or heard their bands perform, but I did not *know* them.

To me, it was disingenuous and dishonest to spend a couple of hours or days interviewing virtual strangers and pretending to know them any better than you. Sure, it would be great to have an excuse to hang out with the greatest minds in our profession, but I was after something more than what you might read in a trade journal. I was interested in the person behind the baton and how it radiated through their teaching. This is why I chose this collection of educators. They are ordinary people who possess extraordinary teaching skills; by understanding not only their traits but the underlying reasons and rationales for the way they work, we can all be better teachers. In the end, I chose them because I admire what they do and who they are. And when all is said and done, I think you will too.

* * *

Many of you have stories to share of equally compelling and amazing teachers; people who have served as mentors, colleagues, and friends. Chances are that as you read these words, you are thinking of one of them. Before continuing, take a moment and reflect on that person. Think about the qualities you admire and want to replicate in your own teaching. Think about the effect that individual had on you as a musician and as a person. Seriously, take a moment and reflect. I will wait...

By spending time with the teachers in this book, I hope to break through the belief that great teaching is something that is unattainable or not trainable. I hope that by reading the stories of nine individuals who have mastered nine important lessons about teaching, you can lessen the perception gap between you and them. These teachers are not perfect; they are subject to hubris and humiliation, just like you. But because we see them through the lens of public performance, we only see a snapshot of who they really are. We see the best and not the rest; we see the performance instead of the process; we see the product and not the person; we see only a small portion of who they really are and try to compare it the complete picture we have of ourselves.

When it comes to excellence in our profession, there is no shortage of people to write about. I am more likely to run out of paper and toner long before I run out of stories. The people in these stories are just a fraction of the thousands of exceptional music educators standing in front of young people each and every day. As you read about them, perhaps it might be worthwhile to think about what a chapter about you would say. After all, you are the *Leader of the Band*.

Enjoy,

Scott

Chapter One

BOBBY KNIGHT AND ME
On humility with Richard Saucedo of Carmel High School

Bobby Knight is one of the most celebrated and simultaneously hated men in sports. He is known as much for his antics as he is his coaching prowess. Born in Ohio in 1940, Bobby was raised by a dictatorial father who helped to shape his hard line approach. Nicknamed "The General," he is feared by some and loathed by many for his unconventional and abusive treatment of his players. In his four decades as a coach, Bobby Knight has amassed more victories (900) than any other Division I coach.

While many have tried to analyze this brilliant and maligned coach, no one has said it better than Hall of Fame coach John Wooden. "People think I don't like him," Wooden said of Knight. "But I don't think there's ever been a better coach than Bobby Knight. Do I like the way he teaches? No, I don't. I never cared for it and I wouldn't want anybody I love to play for Bob Knight."

In a world where winning is paramount, and a state (Indiana) where basketball is a religion, three NCAA titles, an Olympic Gold Medal, and eleven Big Ten

Championships were not enough to save him from himself. His quick temper and aggressive behavior toward players and others finally cost the legendary coach his job. On September 10, 2000, Indiana University President Miles Brand announced he had fired Knight for a continuing pattern of "defiant and hostile" behavior.

> I've got a little class I teach. There are a lot of you who wouldn't like my class. I won't let you come in barefooted. You can't wear a hat. If you cut class, it's an automatic C. And if you cut it twice, you'd better have time to go to Drop and Add.
>
> *- Bobby Knight*

Richard Saucedo loves the man that everyone else loves to hate. As a quiet and unassuming man, Richard has very few passions in his life; his family, his job, flying, and Indiana Basketball, and not necessarily in that order.

"I've learned a ton about teaching from watching Bobby Knight," says Richard.

I was instantly caught off guard by his statement. First, I had no idea Richard even knew what a basketball was, much less what it was used for. Sure, he lives forty minutes north of ground zero for college basketball, but his office contains no memorabilia, pictures, or pennants, and I am not sure that he even *owns* a sweatshirt, much less one from Indiana University. As far as his personal physique, he is far closer to Steve Jobs than Shaquille O'Neal, and

I am fairly convinced he thinks a pick-up game involves playing notes before a measure. I guess I could be wrong. I mean, I can see it now, Richard running up and down the hardwood floor going strong to the hole while talking smack as he schools everyone around him with his A game. Actually, no I can't. This is the antithesis of the man I know. The Richard I know is a gifted pianist, composer, and teacher, but—rabid sports fan?

Even more surprising than Richard's love of basketball is his choice of role models. Sure, he was born and raised in the heart of the Mecca of basketball. And in the Church of Eternal Hardwood, Bobby Knight stands at the pulpit, but—Bobby Knight? If you asked the congregation, it would be an even split between those who consider him a god and those who consider him Satan. It's not his basketball mind that's in question here, it's his basketball soul.

If there were an Olympic event for temper tantrums or chair throwing, Knight would be a sure-fire lock for the gold. If you're hunting for an acerbic and condescending put-down for someone who questions you or your methods, he is the guy you want on your side. Yes, Bobby Knight embodies everything that Richard Saucedo despises, and yet, like a mosquito drawn to a bright blue light, Richard is inexplicably drawn to this person who is seemingly his polar opposite.

I wondered aloud about how would I write a chapter on humility about a man who sees the devil as his idol.

Richard laughed.

> I know that people perceive him that way, but I have learned so much from watching that man. Do you know that when he introduces himself, he calls himself a teacher and not a coach? He doesn't have time for anything but excellence and he is relentless in his pursuit of it.
>
> I have sat behind him on the bench and watched him explode. Granted, it's not always pretty to watch, but I like to take the best from people, and the thing that I take from Bobby Knight is not his maniacal behavior, but the pure teacher in him. I learned from him that you never leave anything to chance when teaching kids. You teach everything you know and then some. Trust me when I say that when you remove the sarcasm from his voice, it's that of a pure teacher.

Richard lights up as he recounts for me the time he met Bobby Knight in person.

> We were filling in for the Indiana University Pep Band during the Hoosier Classic because they were at a football game. The game was a blow out and it was never even close. The team had won, and won big. At the end of the game, just before leaving the floor, Coach Knight passed by

the Carmel band and stopped to thank us for coming. I congratulated him on a good game. He just looked at me and smirked as if to say, "Yeah, right." Even though it was a resounding victory, he knew it was less than the team's best and you could tell he was visibly frustrated. It was one of those *aha* moments, and I remember being profoundly affected by his commitment not to winning, but to teaching and the expectation that we should always give our all, regardless of the competition.

As Richard recounted this story, I wondered if he saw the irony of the situation. How many times have people congratulated him on a performance they found stunning that he believed fell short? How many of Carmel's first place trophies came after lackluster performance? How many times has someone said, "My favorite work of yours is..." and watched him thankfully smile while he tried to hide his dislike for that particular piece? The answer, I suspect, is more often than he would like to admit. And while I am sure that Richard works harder than Knight to filter his responses, he and Bobby have more in common than they might think.

> Listen... what was right twenty-five years ago is still right. I'm not going to change—it's up to them to change. The best teachers I've known are intolerant people. They don't tolerate mistakes.
>
> *- Bobby Knight*

Richard has been teaching at Carmel High School for over twenty-five years. Although there is little tangible evidence of it anywhere in the band room, he has found success in doing it his way for over two and a half decades. Although they have never truly met, and are worlds apart as people, Bobby Knight and Richard Saucedo both share similar personal demons. They are both brooding individuals who are pacified by nothing if not success. Not commercial success, not victories, but the successful moments of teaching and learning that can only occur as a part of the rehearsal process. You get the sense from Richard that the performance process is almost an inconvenience that cuts into his teaching time. He understands its importance to the students and the overall process of teaching and learning, but it is in this tedious place, away from the crowds and surrounded by students that he is most comfortable in his own skin.

* * *

There are people like Bobby Knight who are larger than life, people whose persona is so intense and electric that they steal your attention whether you are a willing participant or not. These people need not speak or make grandiose gestures, as their presence is palpable even to the most unobservant among us. Sometimes known as divas, they need no introduction or gleaming white spotlight to steal the show. They command and demand attention from the very moment they enter. Rare to shy away from the limelight or the pressure associated with it, these people appear so comfortable and confident it is as if they were born to be there. In the world of classical music, these people are often found standing on a podium, waving a little white stick.

In the world of music conductors they are the stars. They are often mocked as being people whose savant-like skills are dwarfed only by their own appreciation for it. But without them, concerts would be far less entertaining and interesting. I suppose it takes a requisite amount of arrogance to command and maintain the attention of 120-plus musicians, not to mention the audience; and I suspect that I am not the only one who is amused by the cartoonesque gesticulations of these characters.

Conductors are often as much a stereotype as they are a leader. Their ragged and ravished snow white hair adrift, these maestros may lack clarity but not conviction. Their dance-like choreography not only controls the music but provides a visual element to an otherwise aural only art form. Rolled into one, these mad geniuses are equal parts Pied Piper, third world dictator, and lead singer from a 1980s hair band. Yes, even in the world of music, there are superstars with egos to match their talent. Special people indeed. This is not Richard Saucedo, who says,

> I am uncomfortable talking to people. I love being around them, but I am uncomfortable just walking up and talking to them. I wish I could make connections with people easier, but I just can't.

As we sit in front of the fireplace on the final morning of the Midwest Clinic, trying to ward off the morning chill, I find it hard to reconcile the words I hear with the man I see. It is especially true given what I am watching unfold in front of my very eyes. In the time it takes Richard to formulate his thoughts and share his self-reflection, no less than three people approach us to speak to him. None of these people have ever met Richard, but they recognize him and are hoping for a little of his time, a slice of his knowledge and a brief story of their brush with greatness. One person is looking for information on composing, one is looking for an honor band clinician, and the final one is just looking to make a connection with someone they admire. As he cradles his hot cocoa (Richard doesn't drink coffee), putting it down only to shake hands, he speaks to each one with the ease and comfort of a skilled politician. I am amused by the irony as I witness someone who pines for people skills interact with total strangers with little effort. As he finishes with the last person, he redirects his attention back to me and says, "Sorry for the interruption... where were we? Oh yeah, I am uncomfortable talking with people..." I just smile and wonder if he sees the same smile from me that he saw from Bobby Knight.

> If you're not careful, you can get a grossly overinflated opinion about your popularity.
>
> *- Bobby Knight*

Richard should be a diva—well, as much a diva as our profession affords. He is at the top of his game, both as a teacher and composer. Given his success, Richard should have an entourage, groupies, and lackeys. I suspect that if you looked hard enough at one of his clinics or followed him around the floor at Midwest, you might find a derivative of all of the above. At the very least, he needs someone who can help clean the pile of paperwork and fast-food wrappers accumulating in his 2002 Ford Escape. If you are wondering how to save the rain forests of Central America, you could start by recycling the contents of his back seat. This vehicle isn't just his mobile office or man-cave, it's some sort of mobile filing system or personal experiment with chaos theory. Given his hectic schedule and status as a father of a toddler, he should have someone who can help him navigate the 150-plus emails he receives each day or someone to sort through his voicemail box that has been full for six months and can no longer accept incoming messages. In this respect he is as much a cartoon character as he is a conductor.

Yes, Richard is at the top of his profession and is entitled to the spoils that come with it. After all, he is a marquee name, both from a teaching and composing standpoint, and his list of accolades and accomplishments are as many and as varied as his trifecta of talent: teaching, composing, and arranging. With over one hundred published works and an equal number of arrangements, he is one of the most sought after people in music education and one of the most prolific composers for the largest publishing company in the world. As if his impressive resume wasn't already impressive enough, in a twelve-month period (2006) he achieved the holy trinity of our profession:

- Music for All Grand National Championship with the Carmel Marching Band
- Drum Corps International World Championship with The Cavaliers
- Performance at the Midwest Clinic with the Carmel Wind Symphony

Yes, in our world, Richard is a rock star, albeit one who is two weeks behind on his bus requests.

Richard is a hard person to truly get to know. Around new people he is guarded and quiet. He does not like crowds and tunes into airport traffic control for relaxation and human interaction. He says that the mindless drone of background conversation provides a way for his mind to rest and relax. I believe the chatter of traffic control provides a temporary pause button for his own thoughts. He listens in to the radio the way he listens in a room full of people, engaged but not involved. I believe this is where he is most comfortable with himself and others. He wants to be a part of the process but not a part of the product. He wants to listen and learn, but not lecture. He wants to hear but not be heard, and yet he is a masterful communicator.

As a composer known for his sophisticated approach to texture and timing, the monotonal and monotonous drone of the control tower allows him to be alone, but not alone. It is hard to reconcile the difference between the man who has a world-class musical ear and the person who prefers the monotony of air traffic control dialog. This is just another example of the duality that is Richard Saucedo, the humble and quiet man who idolizes the egocentric and blustery Bobby Knight. While I cannot fully understand it, I accept it as a part of his persona, as do his colleagues and partners in crime at Carmel High School.

If you were to create a police line-up with his co-directors at Carmel, complete with bright lights and two-way mirror, you would never pick Richard out as the ringleader, and that's the way he likes it. His demeanor and outward appearance are unassuming, unremarkable, and probably better suited to channeling the secret life of Walter Mitty than that of leader and world-class composer. His partners and lifelong friends, Chris Krieke, Andy Cook, and Michael Pote, could all be highly successful head directors at any school in the country, but have made the choice to hang their hats at Carmel. Whether it is out of love for what they do or the people they do it with, this band of brothers has found a way to make amazing music and a fair amount of mischief along the way. Having worked as a team for almost two decades, they teach together year-round, at school, summer camps, and clinics.

You would think that such a talented staff would struggle with the requisite egos that such success brings, but any room that includes the four of them is likely to be among the most ego-free places on the planet. I'm not sure if it's the people, the environment, or the synergy of the two, but these guys are in it together and place a premium on working hard and playing even harder. In the end, they are nothing more than educational junkies in search of their next teaching fix—or practical joke victim, whichever comes along first.

Working as a team for so long has allowed them a such level of comfort and understanding in managing their roles and relationships that they could be the envy of most married couples. They finish each other's sentences and have each other's backs. They each have their strengths and they use them for the good of the students. Think of them as the Three Stooges, with Richard as the innocent camera man they're trying to lure into the onscreen shenanigans who wants nothing of it, and yet gets sucked in anyway.

When I am there, I am often struck by how they have achieved such success in this atypical, non-pressurized atmosphere. There is no grand plan. There are no four-hour management meetings. They do not read books on success and are convinced that Zig Zigler and Steven Covey are a comedy act from the 1950s. There are no discussions of programmatic scope and sequence, and I am fairly certain that if you asked them where their uniforms are stored, they would have to think long and hard before answering the question. While most programs spend months trying to coordinate the musical and visual program, this team takes a far more unconventional approach.

I once asked Chris Kreke about the show design process, and he responded,

> A couple of times we tried to sit down and work through the design process as a team. We spent hours upon hours throwing out ideas and developing a storyboard for our show. We made a huge effort to involve everyone in hope of coming to consensus. As it turned out, those were some

of our worst shows. Our best shows are when Richard says, "Here is what I wrote," and we all sit around a table tossing around ideas on how to build the show around that three minutes of music. When we have an idea, he goes back and finishes the music. I am not saying that's what people should do, but that's what works for us.

Unconventional as their approach may be, they are successful because they are teachers at heart. They teach bell to bell, class to class, and day to day. Bios and job titles are for other people, even though theirs are more lengthy and impressive than most. I doubt that they have business cards, and if they do, I imagine that the only thing they use them for is the lunchtime drawing at their favorite Mexican food joint. They see ego-driven behaviors not as assets, but as impediments to the art of teaching. They are fully engaged in the quest of student development and making music, and realize that no prescribed formula can be the predicate of success.

Just as they have found a unique way of working as a team, they have found an equally unique way of working with kids. They put on no airs. They offer no pretense. They have a deep appreciation and understanding for the delicate balance between planning for future success while living in the current moment. They are truly humble servants to each other and their students. They champion their kids, their sister programs, and every other person in pursuit of perfection, even when it is a rival group.

> You don't play against opponents, you play against the game of basketball.
>
> *- Bobby Knight*

As a matter of routine, I check in with Richard about once a month. Sometimes there is a purpose for the call, sometimes it is just to chat. During my last call I asked him about his upcoming show and how the band was doing. He said,

> We have state championships tomorrow. We're gonna come in third. In fact, we may be the best third place band in the country, and I love it. Everyone around us is getting better and so are we. Our kids are doing great and working their butts off, but you should see *Avon* and *Lawrence Central*, they are really doing well.

And with that, he had shifted the entire conversation to celebrating someone else's accomplishments.

The dictionary defines *humility* as modesty and lacking pretense. A more common definition might include not believing that you are superior to others. Either way it is a double-edged sword. In the world of western philosophy we tend to confuse humility with being weak, meek, or meager. Our culture sees the absence of ego as the absence of power or strength.

An often-practiced view of leadership typically involves a certain amount of ego and arrogance as key components for success. While there is no empirical data that ties ego to productive performance, and conversely hubris to failure, there is a great deal of anecdotal evidence that suggests that the exact opposite is true. Great leaders understand and are able to successfully navigate the balance between these extremes that are required for success and the personal humility to understand their roles within it. Clearly, successful people who are humble do not see themselves as meek or meager. On the contrary, I believe that they see their humility as a source of strength and a necessary component on the pathway to success.

In our society, professional advancement is based in large part on the ability to demonstrate for others our skills and successes. The more we can demonstrate what we can do or produce, the more likely we are to be rewarded with affirmation and the spoils of our profession.

As music teachers, we are no different. We are not adjudicated on how we teach, but how our students perform, which is not always the same. While there is a direct corollary between the quality of teaching and the level of performance, we have all been witness to great technical performances that were lacking in musical substance and or teachable moments—i.e., concerts that were sterile or underprogrammed. Even within a single presentation, a group's performance can change radically based on the literature they play or the conductor on the podium. In our world and in our profession, this "show me" culture of performance-based rewards can create an environment where self-adulation oftentimes trumps self-enlightenment. Additionally, it places us in the difficult situation of being judged based on the final product instead of the process used to achieve it.

Just as one can have an ego without being braggadocio, one can be humble without being self-denigrating. The antithesis of ego is not self-abasement; it's being strong without having to prove it. Richard proves that you can be humble and still value your accomplishments. Hubris is at the epicenter of our need to be prideful, but as professional educators, we need to contain our pride within the framework of its true importance and temper it with recognition of those who helped us in the process.

Excessive or arrogant pride often blinds us to reality and sacrifices our perspective for a greater feeling of self-worth or importance. True humility not only requires true achievement, but also the ability to not tie it to self-worth. Confidence is best displayed through our ability to control it and use it in a manner of strength and not aggressiveness. Richard is able to navigate between the desire to do what is right and his need to be recognized for it artfully, keeping the two in balance.

"I have as much of an ego as anyone else," Richard says as he sips his hot chocolate, "but ego is not what makes us successful, passion is."

> Ego... well, I am not sure what ego is, but I don't have a lot of time to deal with it. The day is just so busy that you don't have a lot of time to think about it. But when I do, I do my best to tame it. As I get a better handle on how to deal with my own ego, I can see where I have come from and how much I have around me, and frankly, I am

just trying not to blow it. When I was a young band director, I was *way* more stupid that I am now, and that is saying something. It was more about me than the kids. I yelled a lot, and I mean a *lot*!

In retrospect, it seems that the more I yelled, the worse the group got. The worse they got, the more I yelled. After awhile, I realized that I was talking too much and not listening enough. The more I listened to my groups, the better they got. What gives me joy is being totally connected and in the moment with the people around me, even if nothing is being said. You can't connect when you are the only one communicating. This is what I think music education is about, connecting and communicating.

It's hard to ignore the profoundness of his thoughts and the honesty with which he shares them. He is willing to reveal not only his successes, but his failures as well. He will share them with anyone who asks. He is painfully honest about his shortcomings and transparent in his philosophies. This does not minimize what he has accomplished, but rather allows him to appreciate it.

I'd be less than honest if I didn't say to myself, "What am I doing this for?"

- Bobby Knight

Away from school, Richard Saucedo is a man who appears at times to be uncomfortable in his own skin. It is as if his success as a composer and clinician has left him somewhat adrift at sea without a paddle. The demands placed on him by publishers, those who commission him, and his role as a department chair are all waves pushing against his boat, keeping him from making the progress towards his true port and some much-needed rest. He is a reluctant slave to his workload, but even more restless when given the freedom of an unscheduled day. To him, this is just empty space waiting to be filled with another opportunity, like learning to fly. Richard needs to be challenged. He needs to be occupied. He needs every facet of his personality to be engaged, even if it means being simultaneously pulled in many different directions. He needs mental and physical activity like he needs chatter from air traffic control. For Richard, a mind in motion is a mind at peace, and a mind at rest is a mind in conflict.

When you watch Richard teach, there is nothing extraordinary about what he does, but when he is done, the summation of what he has accomplished is amazing. It is as if he is performing an educational slight of hand trick. You see everything he is doing, hear everything he is saying, but when all is said and done, you can't describe how he did it, much less replicate it.

Bell to bell, Richard is focused, calm, and consistent. He would no sooner ride the high of the moment than he would ride the low. To the untrained or unobservant among us, his classes are uneventful, if not boring. He is a funny person, but uses humor sparingly. He is an insightful person, but prefers for the students to figure it out for themselves. He is a composer and teacher who writes for his own band, but leaves the interpretation to his staff. His willingness to be a part of but not own the entire process is one of the many reasons he and his groups have been so successful.

> I am proud of what we have done at Carmel and how we are perceived by those around the country and the world. But I am such a small part of it. My colleagues and students who do so much to make it happen are what make the activity and my memories so special.

But there is nothing special about them or Richard. Every August I spend two days working with the entire Fine Arts Department at Carmel. Keep in mind, a fine arts faculty meeting at Carmel consists of four band directors, one percussion teacher, two orchestra directors, three theatre teachers, three choir directors, a piano/technology teacher, and two full-time theatre tech coordinators. This doesn't include the department secretary or the part time/itinerant staff associated with the marching band. As I said, this is a place that defies the national trends that show declining enrollment in public school music programs. Despite the sheer number of kids involved, you would not classify the music students of Carmel as overtly or excessively talented. They are not prodigies who wander the hallways listening to Cage or Schoenberg on their iPods. The do not argue the merits of the twelve-tone matrix during their lunch break. They are not breaking down practice room doors to hone their techniques, and the staff is the first to admit that they lack a formal private lesson program.

Marching band is optional and requires no audition. As long as you are willing to make the time commitment, you are in the group, and anyone who sees the group in August can attest that when they say anyone, they mean anyone. The students in the Carmel Band are worried about prom, boyfriends, makeup, parents, grades, and yes, when pushed by the staff, their music. In short, there is little which differentiates the Carmel band room from any of the other twenty-thousand band rooms in the United States. But from the moment these students join band, they are taught first and foremost that they are a part of something bigger and more important than just themselves. Richard says,

> We are fortunate to have what we have and are reminded of that on an almost daily basis. In our department, we are working on a special project right now called the Ugandan Project. We paired up with an inner-city school in New York City to raise enough money to build a school for people who have nothing. These are kids who watched their parents die and then had to be the ones to dig the hole and bury them. Through it all, the death and destruction, they celebrate and grieve through music. I think these people and that part of the world is about to teach us an important lesson about the power of music.

> A player enters the Hall of Fame on his ability. A coach enters on the ability of his players.
>
> *- Bobby Knight*

We try to teach the kids that success is what you make it out to be and it is defined on your terms. The year after we won Grand Nationals, we placed eighth. I cannot tell you how many people called to tell us how bad they felt that we had placed so low. What they did not know was that we had over eighty freshmen marching that year. From day one, we explained this to the kids that this was going to be a year where we measured success not with awards, but with personal and musical growth. Privately, I felt that we would not even make it to finals and really had no business even thinking about it. Even though the group lacked the accolades of previous years, it turned out to be one of our best years ever. We achieved so much more than when we actually won the year before.

Don't get me wrong, it was nice to win Grand Nationals, and I don't see competition as a bad thing. Competition helps; the kids need external motivation, whether we want to admit it or not. But there is a difference between wanting to win and wanting to beat someone else. We stress that a lot with our students. Yes, competition is a part of life, but we don't ask the Chicago Symphony and the Los Angeles Philharmonic to compete. They both exist to achieve independent of one another. When it comes to winning, we remind the kids that we have lost far more often than we have won and that we do not exist to win, we exist to achieve!

For years I have wrestled with the issue of competition and how to best harvest its benefits while acknowledging its potential problems. I once had a conversation with a well respected and thoughtful colleague who shared his belief that ego was not only important but was in fact a necessary component of success. To his way of thinking, personal ego was the driving force behind our wanting to do better as people and as professionals. He felt that personal investment and ego were inexorably intertwined, and without either, you could not achieve optimum results. Our society fosters this type of thought process. We see *ego* as a by-product of success, but when you look it up in the dictionary, this is what you get:

e•go |ˈēgō|
noun (pl. **egos**) self-esteem, self-importance, self-worth, self-respect, self-image, self-confidence.

Notice that the one word that appears over and over is *self*. The dominant force of ego-driven achievement is rooted in one's own accomplishments. This isn't necessarily wrong, but it presents obstacles when also rooted in the communal setting of band. In music education, ego becomes dangerous when we use our program as a vehicle to fulfill or measure our sense of self-worth. While our success as teachers and those of our students are deeply intertwined and can often be met simultaneously, too often we place our ego in front of the best interests of our students. These are times when the hierarchy of priorities can become clouded and misguided. As teachers, when our own ego is involved in making educational decisions, we are more likely to make and justify poor choices. Our ego is our 24/7/365 companion and is as much a part of our success as it is our failure. The tipping point in either direction is how you use it. When balanced towards self-serving interests, students are quick to sniff it out; and no amount of success will disguise your true intent.

* * *

As music educators there are many ways that our ego participates in the educational process. Have you ever allowed your ego to color your judgment when programming for a concert or festival? Think about it; haven't we all chosen a piece of literature that we wanted to conduct but the ensemble was not ready to play? Have you ever used your students' success as an measuring stick of *your* success? Have you ever entered a specific event or contest because you knew your group was more likely to place higher or win more awards? Do you introduce yourself as a Director of Bands rather than a music teacher? Have you ever heard a science teacher introduce themselves as Director of Scientific Studies? No! The fact is, our ego plays a more significant role in our day-to-day operations than we might think. This is neither positive nor negative, it just is. How we allow our egos to alter what we do and why we do it can create problematic situations. Our egos are attention-seeking adrenaline junkies in search of their next audience.

As a rule, music educators are more personally invested in their students' success than their non-musical colleagues. Their skills sets as performers are directly related to how successful they are perceived as teachers. We arrive early, stay late, sacrifice our weekends, and spend our entire summer planning for the coming year. Few, if any other curricula demand this level of commitment from teachers. With such strong passions and so little time, the lines between professional and personal become blurred. Our friends are our colleagues. Our professional experiences are blurred with our personal interests. Even our free time and leisure activities serve as only a brief respite between work-related thoughts. Consider this: Have you ever gone to a concert to relax? Have you ever gone to a college football game just to see the band? Have you ever planned a vacation around a drum corps show or summer music event? Have you ever attended a convention and considered it a vacation?

With such a blurring between the lines of the professional and personal, many educators have allowed their personal sense of self-worth and ego to be intertwined with their professional lives. For some, the barometer of self-appreciation rises and falls with the successes and failures not of self, but of their students. Rooted in perspective, this means that you have attached your own sense of value to something of which you have only limited control—a dangerous proposition indeed. Beyond that, the lines have been blurred between what is best for you and what is best for the students. Add to this the fact that the greatest source of professional feedback comes through the lens of an adjudicator who is in the business of evaluating our students' performance, and you can see where we have set ourselves up for a problematic situation. Saucedo says,

> I am happy coming to work. I genuinely enjoy working with our kids, perhaps more so now than ever. I am fortunate enough to be able to travel and work with many groups in various places and genres, but my favorite moments happen when I'm standing in the Carmel band room, in front of Carmel kids.

As you look at the walls of your office or your rehearsal space, take an inventory of how each individual memento makes you feel. The artifacts and photos in Richard's cavernous office remind you of the obstacles overcome and goals achieved in his two and a half decades at Carmel.

In rehearsal spaces large and small, urban and suburban, items like these are usually abundant in nature and prominently displayed. They are both a measurement of and a testament to the work that has been done and the success that you and your students have achieved. Take inventory of this moment and the feelings that you have. Try to absorb the depth and warmth of what you are feeling as you look at these objects. You are more than likely feeling a sense of pride.

Now return to that same space and look for the things that bring you joy. Look for things that make you smile, warm your heart, and move you. These may be the same objects you viewed before, but your response to them should be different. Both emotional, yes, but they evoke emotions in very different ways. These items signify seminal moments and people that require no validation from an external panel of judges. These are moments that require no participation from our ego for us to feel good. They validate and balance the ego. They are indicators not of the world's view of us, but of our view of the world.

Pride gives us a sense of self-worth and importance. Joy gives us a sense of self-fulfillment. Both are necessary, but maybe they should not be quite so intertwined. Perhaps we should focus more on the moments and people that give us joy. People that inspire us to create not only a better program but a better self. The rehearsal room can and should be a place that inspires students to look forward and not back; a place for all to be reminded about not only what has transpired but what is expected. Or maybe, just maybe, a place filled with joy is all that is required to create something to be proud of. Things that make us proud create opportunities. Things that give us joy make us human.

> Hell, I don't even watch the pros. If the NBA was on Channel 5 and a bunch of frogs making love were on Channel 4, I'd watch the frogs—even if they came in fuzzy.
>
> *- Bobby Knight*

Like Knight, Richard has had plenty of opportunities to leave Carmel High School and teaching in general. His success as a teacher and composer has all but put a target on his back. And to add fuel to the fire, he is already eligible to retire, having taught over thirty years. He has been approached by colleagues, colleges, and businesses alike to "make the leap," but leap he does not. Through it all, he seems firmly ensconced in the same job he has held for over twenty-five years. His life would be easier if he were to be able to focus on just one thing. He would certainly have more time at home with his wife, Sarah, and children, Carmen and Ethan. I believe he fears the unknown. Not of what or how he would fill his time, but of who he would become and how he would be remembered. Just as we all do, Richard has wrapped a portion of his personal identity into his job, but not in the way you might think.

One of the first things I notice when I walk into the band room at Carmel High is that the walls are remarkably barren. If you did not know the impressive history of this storied program, you might think you were in the presence of organization that has achieved absolutely nothing. The lack of anything historical or significant adorning the walls is almost as overwhelming as the knowledge of what could and should be there. It is as if the program itself was completely devoid of ego and identity. There is nothing in the room other than what is required to teach and learn: chairs, stands, a chalk board and a sound system. Everything else comes from the students and teachers. As I stood in that empty room, wondering where it all was, the bell rang and in came the students, and immediately I found it. I felt the joy of the Carmel Band program.

Richard's favorite Bobby Knight story involves a pointed exchange in which a player struggling in practice was hit by a basketball on the side of the head. Even though he was in a full contact drill, he had fallen, unaware of his teammates and what was going on. After the coach blew the whistle, stopping the drill, the tension was immediately palpable. The lapse of focus was something the ill-tempered coach was not likely to excuse without a dose of humiliation. As the team nervously looked on, Bobby Knight calmly walked up the player and said, "Son, if you stay in the game long enough, *eventually* someone will pass you the ball. So be aware and expect the best."

I do believe Richard has been in the game long enough and is aware. I know for sure that he expects the best each and every day. Richard says,

> We have so much more to do at Carmel. We need a private lesson program. We don't do enough chamber music and we don't do near enough leadership… and once, just once, I want to run a *great* rehearsal. There is a lot more that needs to be done.

And in that one sentence I saw it. Right there in front of me, after three hours of searching, I found it. In that moment, I saw his inner Bobby Knight shining through. I'm just glad that the chair he was sitting in was too big for him to throw at me.

Chapter Two

Mac vs PC and The Attack of the Killer Tomatoes

On finding your fit with David Duarté of the Deer Valley Unified School District

I hate Macs. I have always hated Macs. I hate people who use Macs. I even hate people who don't use Macs but sometimes wish they did. Macs are glorified Fisher Price activity centres for adults; computers for scaredy-cats too nervous to learn how proper computers work; computers for people who earnestly believe in Feng Shui.

Charlie Brooker
The Guardian Newspaper
February 5, 2007

Mac users swear by their computers. PC users swear at their computers.

Anonymous

There are many cultural divides in our profession, country, and world; serious issues that define us as professionals and people. Race, politics, religion, and government are just a few of the issues filled with venomous rhetoric and heartfelt beliefs. The discourse is usually invested more in reaffirming our current beliefs than in convincing someone else. Liberal versus conservative, rich versus poor, and Democrat versus Republican are just a few of the many identities people hold dear. While significantly less important, just as deeply embedded and viscerally fought are the two camps of computer users: those who prefer Apple, Inc.'s Macintosh (a.k.a. Mac users) and devotees of machines that run Microsoft Windows (PC users). No other device, electronic or otherwise, has sparked greater interest among users and within the American psyche. Not since Coke versus Pepsi in the early 1980s have we seen the general public invest so heavily in a brand name war. Few if any of us have the knowledge or skills sets to be able to make an empirical or logical argument as to why one machine is better than another. And yet, with a fervency usually reserved for the evangelical, we stand devout in our belief that we are right, and our computer is better.

At the epicenter of this great divide stand two onetime friends and now competitors: Apple CEO Steve Jobs and Microsoft Founder, Bill Gates. They are as different as their machines and as iconic as any two business people in America. One is considered thoughtful and reflective, the other, brash and outspoken; one in khakis and a button-down, the other in a black mock turtleneck and jeans; one trying to save the world, the other trying to change it. Yes, they are as different as night and day, rain and sun, winter and summer; and yet both are vibrant and successful world leaders in the same industry. How did they do it? They found their fit.

* * *

David Duarté is the very definition of a man in search of the perfect fit. Having been a duck out of water many times, he now truly understands the need for each of us to be comfortable in our surroundings and in our own skin. I first met David fifteen years ago. Someone recommended him to me as an up-and-coming music arranger and young teacher. I needed someone who could produce a couple of arrangements quickly, as our ensemble had been selected to perform at the MENC Biennial Conference, and I wanted to use the Canadian Brass as guest artists. This required someone who could arrange for world-class musicians and high school students with equal ease. It also required someone who could translate the classic brass quintet sound into the jazz idiom. And I needed the arrangement *fast*! David's knowledge of jazz and brass coupled with his intellect and computer prowess made him the perfect man for the job. Keep in mind, back in 1997, computers were still a relatively new tool in the writing of music and drill. Despite his youth, he could work a computer like a piano, and make virtual music faster than anyone I had ever seen. Being a fellow Mac-o-phile and novice computer geek, he became my go-to guy when I had a question, problem, or inadvertent computer freeze.

Over the years, as both of our careers unfolded we became more than colleagues; we became friends. Occasionally we would share a drink, a meal, and a teaching tip. We saw each other at football games, conferences, and the occasional pool party. To get a call or email from David was not an unusual event in my day, week, or month, until I became an administrator. The same year I made the jump from the classroom, David made the jump to a new school. As you can imagine, the increased workload and new environments kept us both busy and somewhat out of touch, which made the phone call that year all the more surprising and welcome.

Shari Olsen (my secretary) came into my office holding the same three colored manila folders she handed me every morning. Sorted by their contents, she quickly and quietly briefed me on the folders and the day's events. Anyone who has ever worked in a high school knows that the administrative assistants run the school, and Shari was no exception. She had survived many an administrator before me, and I knew deep down that she would outlast me as well. It's no secret among teachers that the two people you need to have on your side and on your speed dial are the principal's secretary and the head custodian.

Shari was polite, demure, and extremely detail oriented. She was long on people skills and short on disorganization. She was the queen of the roost in the activities office long before I took over, and given her tenure of service, I think she saw me as more of a squatter than a boss. She was my rock. She tamed the chaos and put things in order. She provided me with structure and a to-do list every day. I not only appreciated it, I depended upon it. This was my five minutes of quiet before the storm, and while I knew not what lay in front of me, a storm was a certainty. As she drew her morning briefing to a close, she told me that I had a call holding on line one.

Despite my best efforts to hide it, it was no secret to anyone who knew me as a teacher that I was unhappy as an assistant principal. I tried to put on a game face, but... let's just say I would make a lousy poker player. You might think that a master's degree in administration, a sixty-hour internship, and a four-month stint as an interim assistant principal would have given me more than an adequate glance and prepared me for what administrative life would entail, but somehow it hadn't. Either I had blinders on or was a very slow student. After all of that work I found myself totally unprepared for the daily assault on my professional self-esteem that accompanied my new position.

As a band director I enjoyed my job. I looked forward to going to work and I enjoyed working with young people. But just seven months into my new position, neither of these things was true anymore. The minutes and hours of my day were filled with students who did not care about learning and made no attempt to disguise it. Where I once spent my days making music with the brightest of young people, I was now relegated to spending time with one hundred and seventy-five pounds of Camel cigarette reeking apathy. I know this because after time, I had learned to differentiate the smell of various smoking products, both legal and otherwise.

Looking back, I am struck by how quickly I lost my idealism and settled into the pragmatic if not hopeless approach of "No matter what I do, he will be back in that same chair tomorrow for the same offense." The passion that attracted me to the profession like a thousand-pound magnet was now repelling me with equal force. This was a foreign feeling to me. I had spent more than a decade happily working in public schools, and now felt lost and hopeless. I had never felt that before. I knew that if I didn't make the change back to the classroom quickly, I would be gone from the profession forever. I was ready for a change, but was not sure how it would present itself and where I would end up.

"This is Scott Lang, can I help you?" I said, feigning sincerity.

Let's be honest; people only call an assistant principal when they are angry. And the worst part is that so often, there is little I can do to help. Given that fact, fifty percent of what I just said was a lie. I was in fact Scott Lang, but there was little chance that I could really help the caller. I avoided the phone like the plague. The red blinking message light was now my nemesis, my combatant in the daily war to save my sanity. If it were not for Shari working the front lines and taking the bullet of the first assault, I don't know what I would have done.

"Hey Scott, this is David. How are you?"

When I moved to the front office, David moved to a successful program at a sister school in my district that recently had been through a fair amount of turmoil. How funny that, after years of knowing each other, he entered into my district just as I had exited the classroom. In the many hours we spent together, we often talked about what it would be like to work collaboratively, and just as I accepted a position in the front office, he accepted a position at the high school down the street.

"I heard you were thinking about getting back into the game. What's going on?" David asked.

I explained that I wasn't happy coming to work every day, and that as much as I knew I needed more time to become acclimated to the job, I was equally convinced that if I committed to another year of the helpless and hapless, I would be too far gone to return to education in any form. I also explained that as bad as I felt for leaving my school of over ten years in a lurch, remaining an administrator was not an option.

"So what are you going to do?"

I told him that I had interviewed for a position at a new school on the north side of town and was getting ready to meet with them for a second interview and possibly an offer. The thought of replacing my four-minute commute with a forty-five-minute commute was somewhat tempered by the excitement of creating something from nothing. I had met with the administrative team, called fellow directors from that district, and spent some time talking with teachers at the feeder schools. The situation was far from ideal, and

I knew it would be years before this new program would reach the height of the one I had just left, if ever. But it was a job, and it was better than the one I was currently occupying.

"When are you meeting with them?" he asked.

"Later today," I said.

"Are you going to be in your office for the next hour or so?" He asked.

Curious as to why he would ask, I answered, "Yes, why?"

"Just stay there until you hear from me," he responded and then hung up the phone.

For lack of anything better to think about, my mind raced with possibilities. Was he coming over? Was something wrong? What was going on?

I was almost immediately drawn back from my daydreaming by the harshness of the morning bell, and with it the stream of recalcitrant students who began to arrive. That morning in particular contained nothing unusual: ditching, smoking, cursing, graffiti, blah, blah, blah. As I became immersed in pushing paper, calling parents, and following up with teachers, I completely forgot about my earlier conversation with David. As welcome of an interlude as it was, the immediacy of a packed outer office did not afford me the luxury of an indulgent thought or mental reprieve.

In-between student interviews Shari stuck her head in the doorway and said, "You have a call on line one, a David Duarté. Do you want to take it?"

Anxious for a resolution and eager for a diversion, I said, "Yes," and grabbed the phone.

"Scott... this is David," he said with an almost audible smirk.

"What's going on, David?" I responded, trying to sound nonchalant.

"You need to stay by your phone for the next fifteen minutes," he said.

My mind started racing through the reasons for receiving an important phone call and what might be happening. Knowing that it was not likely to be a call from Publishers Clearing House, I began to filter out the absurd and focus in on the reality.

"Is everything okay?" I asked.

"It is now," he said with an almost auditory sense of relief. And then he began to fill in the blanks.

"Steve Adolph, the Principal here, is about to call you and offer you the job as Director of Bands. I just walked up to the front office and resigned. I told him all about you and he was excited. He should be calling you within the next fifteen minutes."

"What? How? Why?" But before I could get the words out, he finished the story.

"I'm not happy here. I'm not sure if I even want to teach anymore. I may go back to school and get a performance degree, or I may just leave education all together. I'm not sure... but I *am* sure that I won't be back here next year."

Being an administrator had left me out of the loop and unaware that David had struggled in his new position.

He was more than capable and competent to stand in front of any group, but he had underestimated the anger of the students after losing their director of two decades as well as his resolve to weather the ensuing storm. As unfortunate as the situation was, the fractured state of the program, his ego, and the students' sense of purpose had made this inevitable. The administrators were now daily observers in the classroom, trying to hold at bay a group that was bent on self-destruction.

It slowly began to sink in as I thought about the difficult challenges of being the third director in three years at a sister high school. While any seasoned teacher or outside observer would look at this as a questionable move, I saw this as an escape from the four walls of the office that had become my prison; and as any prisoner will tell you, when you have been locked up for eight months, any escape is a good one.

As I began to wrap my arms and my mind around what was unfolding, Shari stuck her head in once again and said, "You have a call on line two, it's Steve Adolph, the Principal at Marcos. Do you want to take the call?"

Hearing the conversation through the phone, David responded for me, "Take the call, Scott. And congratulations. You'll be a good fit for this program."

Those last eight words still ring in my ears today.

* * *

David Duarté is a bundle of attention deficit energy best described as a chipmunk after drinking a multi-shot cappuccino. As uncomfortable as he is with lack of motion, he is equally uncomfortable with silence. There are those who think and then talk; David talks in order to think. It's his way of processing information. He likes to hear ideas out loud and then judge their merit or accuracy. He hears thoughts more clearly than he sees them. He sees concepts better than he reads them. He plays things better than he describes them. David is a one-man, multimedia, multitasking machine. He is a sight to behold and entertaining to spend time with. He is bright, personable, engaging, articulate, funny, and I imagine was his own worst nightmare as a band director.

David is at his happiest when there is some semblance of chaos. He neither requires nor relishes structure, and yet is able to see and maintain it in almost everything he does. He is able to juggle many different things at once and place them in such a hierarchy that he deals only with the balls that are about to be dropped. To his way of thinking, all other things can wait. His email inbox is overflowing to the point of overwhelming, but David sees it as a comforting sign that he belongs and is needed. This is his place in the world—the place where he thrives.

"I'm the laziest hard-working person, or the hardest-working lazy person you will ever meet," he says. "I'm not sure which I am or which is better, but there I am. I get done what needs to be done in real time as it needs to be done. It's not because of procrastination, but because that is the way my mind works. I am always in the moment... the here and now, even when I should be thinking about the there and then."

After resigning from Marcos David took the next three months to simultaneously ponder and prepare for his new future. He applied to grad school, downsized his lifestyle, and began to look for new directions in his life. He had narrowed his search to a couple of different options within music education, but being a high school teacher was not one of them. As far as he was concerned, whatever door opened first would be the door he would walk through. Although just a few months earlier he had sworn he was done, opportunity and need came calling to entice him to return. The week before band camp a local school lost its director and was desperately trying to find someone to fill a very big void.

> The principal at Deer Valley High School had lost her director the week before band camp. Asking around about available teachers, she heard about me and begged me to come teach her band camp. She said it would be just one week and would give her time to find a permanent replacement. I said yes out of guilt for a band program with no director and told her that I would stay on until they found someone else. When I showed up at Deer Valley, I was the third band director in as many months. I was such a bad fit at my previous job and had had such a negative experience that I was basically burned out as a teacher. I didn't even want to go back to public education. I had committed myself to head back to grad school and pursue higher education.

I thought it would be a week, two at most, but little did I know she had a plan in place to hold on to me. After her third attempt to convince me to stay, she asked me, "What would it take to get you to stay?"

That is a question few teachers will ever be asked, and I wasn't about to pass up the opportunity to answer. I told her I would think about it and get back to her. Can you imagine getting that question? If you did, would you be prepared to answer it on the spot? The next day I walked into her office with a list of requirements that included a better salary, new instruments, technology, and a supply budget that would show she was serious about her band program. It never crossed my mind that she would agree. Three days later, I signed my contract. As I left her office, we both felt good. She had staved off chaos for one more year and I had only committed myself to another nine months of teaching.

That first year was as good as the previous year was bad. I started with seventy kids, built the number up to 110, started two jazz bands, and got the kids to start buying into me and my system. My new students were not nearly as talented as those at my previous job, but I learned the hard way that talent alone doesn't make a teacher happy.

The job was hard, but I was able to shake that off because I never saw myself being there for the long haul. I just figured that whatever success we had was gravy, and that no matter what I did, I was better than the alternative of no teacher. I'm not saying that I didn't take it seriously; I guess I just didn't take it *too* seriously. I really think that it made a difference, and after the first year when I was asked to return, I did. I was surprised that as the program kept progressing, my enthusiasm for teaching was returning as well. I began to feel the passion to teach again. My new home just fit me, as a person and as a teacher.

When I asked David how important "fit" is in teaching, he said:

For me personally, I learned the hard way that fit is a huge part of success. How you react to the various situations and surroundings says a lot about you as a person. I was surprised that the places that I fit best were places where the school community matched where I was raised. Honestly, while the musicians were not as accomplished or successful, it was where I was the happiest. I learned that you can't change who you are or where you come from.

If you were raised and now live in one environment and work in another without

> taking a long hard look at yourself, then you might just be asking for trouble. This applies to academics, demographics, socioeconomics, and even to location. What I learned was that I should have looked at everything else first. What I saw was the quality of the group and not the environment in which they operated. Had I looked at the culture first and quality second, I would have never even applied for that job at Marcos de Niza.

There is an unspoken understanding in music education that the better your ensembles play, the better teacher you are. It's never discussed out loud nor is it debated in academia, but it is the unspoken law of the land. We also correlate the quality of the performance with the level of job satisfaction. When looking at music programs, we assume with our ears instead of seeing with our eyes and asking with our words. It is a kind of like musical blinders that leave us listening to what is happening on the outside rather than the voice on the inside. I asked David if he had been a victim of this.

> Yes... I suppose to a degree that is true. When I went to Marcos de Niza, I saw the history, performance quality, and a level of support from the community that I wasn't used to. It was nothing like my high school experience or any place I had taught previously. I was from a different part of the valley, a place where kids had no sense of belonging and parents didn't even

come to concerts, much less booster meetings. It was the direct opposite of what I walked into at Marcos. I was a stranger to them as a person and as a teacher. We had almost nothing in common. More than that, I was the wrong fit for them—not as a musician, but as a program director and educational leader.

They were looking for guidance, but I walked in and wanted to provide a structure that they did not need or welcome. They had that in place already. They weren't interested in changing that part of the program. By and large, they were happy with what they had created and weren't looking for a fresh perspective; they wanted the same. When I went to Deer Valley I was able to do what I do best, which is to provide structure for those students who need and crave it. I had found a place that needed what I could offer on all levels. We were matching pieces of the puzzle that needed each other to create the bigger picture.

I think that the fastest way to be successful is to ensure that the job fits you, as it is much harder to change yourself to fit the job. I found I was most successful when I taught in the places that needed the skills I already had. This comes from who you are, not how you were trained. You are a product of your environment and upbringing in addition to your training.

I asked David if his fit has changed as he has matured as a teacher.

> I think it absolutely did. While I don't believe that you can run from the essence of who you are, you do change as a person and a professional with experience and time. In the beginning, as teachers and program directors, more than learning our craft, we have to learn who we are, what we are capable of, and how to reconcile the two. There is no way to teach this; you just have to experience it for yourself.
>
> As professionals we have to plan, budget, organize, meet, communicate, work with administration, work with parents, and serve as a substitute janitor and bus driver in our spare time. These tasks can be taught, but learning about where we fit in this profession and in the world is something we have to experience. For those who pay attention to their inner voice, the lesson can be learned quickly. But when your cognitive dissonance and ego get in the way, the journey becomes significantly longer and more difficult.
>
> What I have learned is that whether or not we are successful in this profession is as much a part of who we are as what we have been trained to be.

As these words came out of David's mouth, I could not help but think of the old child development argument of nature versus nurture. I wondered: How much of our success as music educators is predetermined? Are we genetically molded to be better at teaching at the secondary or elementary level? And are some of us are naturally better suited to deal with certain types of student groups?

I think it is well accepted that some people possess greater physical or genetic gifts in music and am curious to know if the same holds true for teaching. How much of who we are as teachers stems from who we are as people versus how we learned our craft? While I doubt that anyone would argue that it is completely nature or nurture, I suspect that there is significant disagreement about where the balance between the two lies. We all have certain personal characteristics that enable or impede us in being more or less successful in certain situations, such as patience, drive, passion, temperament, and so on. So how much of each is required for success?

Think about it. If you are someone who is naturally organized, a strong communicator, and feels comfortable in the public eye, you may be more successful as a head director or in a large program than someone who lacks those same skill sets, even though they may possess equal or even greater podium skills. Is someone with a more nurturing personality going to be more successful in the elementary setting than someone who lacks those people skills but has better pedagogy? When teaching in the inner city, is it more important to have the right personality or musical training?

The same types of questions can be asked about where in the system we decide to teach. We often choose a level of education (elementary, secondary, or collegiate) based on our musical desires and skills rather than our personal ones. Some people are more intuitive to the needs and ways of certain age levels, thus making their personal skills more important than their musical abilities. Perhaps when it comes to music educators, we should be administering personality tests in addition to music theory exams. After all, a twelve-tone matrix is of little importance to someone who seeks to teach *Go Tell Aunt Rhodie*.

"We are patterned people," says David. "You can change, but you can't run from you who are. You are who you are."

When I prodded him to expand, he said,

> Teachers need to be more honest with themselves about who they are and what they can offer. They need to look at what they are successful at and what they are not. Success and failure are patterns, and to ignore them is asking for a disaster.
>
> Knowing what I know now, I should have never applied for that job at Marcos. I should have seen and known that the situation there was not a good fit. I am not sure if it was the situation, the job, or me, but the writing was there on the wall; I just didn't read it. I was ignorant to the

fact that not everyone wants to learn from the same person and in the same way. I took the job because everything was in place: equipment, facilities, musicians, history, etc.

I do best when taking over situations in chaos. I thrive on the challenge and appreciate the fact that I am needed. I see it now as a pattern. It is a personality trait. I should have known this earlier, but I did not want to believe it. In order to know it, we have to own it first.

As a profession, music teachers and teachers in general are enablers, and I am the king of them. We help each other cover our weaknesses rather than confront and correct them. In my role as a district arts coordinator *(a position David assumed in 2010)* I am no different. I spend a lot of time helping the music teachers in my district cover and recover from their mistakes, not become better instructional leaders. This not only masks the problems but also enables the person to continue to operate without addressing or correcting it. This is something I am working on as I learn to be a better leader.

Once you step back and look at the larger picture, it's easier to see because we're in the profession of helping people. But sometimes we help too

> much. We fail our music teachers by not allowing them to fail. We allow them to continue in situations where they are not successful because we don't want them to *feel* unsuccessful. We refuse to speak with candor and be forthright in the name of kindness.

I asked David for an example.

> Honestly, certain people should not be in front of certain ensembles. They have neither the skill sets nor personality to be successful in front of a class.

He paused.

> To be honest, I think there are a great many teachers who are not just in the wrong place; they are in the wrong profession. Some of these people should not be teaching at all. We have confused loving music with loving to teach music, and I am not convinced they are the same love.

When I asked him how many teachers he thought were either in the wrong fit or the wrong career, he responded, "My experience tells me too many of them."

When I pressed him on what percentage were in the wrong situation versus wrong profession, he just smiled and asked me how my sandwich was.

He has a point. I have often wondered if we are

attracting the wrong type of people to be music educators. For example, if you love math, you become a mathematician. If you love history, you become a historian. If you love science, you become a scientist, and when you do so, there is reason to believe that where you had success in high school, you will have similar success in college and your career.

But music education is different. In music, it is a love of the curricula combined with a love of the experience of making music *and* teaching others to make music. When you ask someone to recount their favorite parts of their high school ensemble experience, more often than not they talk about the process and not the product. They talk about trips, rehearsals, memories, and friends, not just the music. Many music education majors are looking for an unnatural extension of their own high school experiences only to find that teaching provides very few of these opportunities.

Is it possible that the very qualities that make this activity so attractive to young people are not the same qualities that will make them successful at leading it? Is it possible that, in addition to not being honest with themselves, music education professionals as a group have not been honest with them, either? Is it possible that the very kids who would be the most successful as music teachers are choosing to become doctors, lawyers, and scientists? Is it possible that we are attracting people who are seeking an avocation (a pursuit of something they love) rather than those who see it as a vocation? Loving music makes you a music aficionado; loving kids makes you empathetic; but neither makes you a great teacher. This is the message that I believe we have failed to convey to our future educators.

* * *

If fit is so important, then questions emerge. Would Bill Gates have been successful working in the counter-corporate culture of Apple? Would Steve Jobs have been a failure in the more prototypical structure at Microsoft? No one would argue whether they are smart enough; but success is something all together different. Acumen and intellect alone are not enough to guarantee success.

In what was a shock to all, after seemingly irrational and distracting behavior seen as antithetical to the culture of American business, Apple, Inc. founder Steve Jobs was ousted in 1985. The brash persona which helped him rise to the top, later served to send him to the bottom. He was seen as no longer fitting in at the company he had helped to create.

In the book *Outliers*, author Malcolm Gladwell argues that success is best achieved when we marry opportunity and talent—that neither unto itself is enough to achieve and sustain greatness. To illustrate the point, he details the education and rise to prominence of Microsoft founder Bill Gates. In an eloquent and acerbic way, Gladwell explains that while he doesn't dispute the intellectual prowess of this international tech star, he believes that without the unique and inexplicable collision of circumstance and opportunity Bill Gates would never have achieved the level of greatness that he is known for today.

It turns out that Gates went to the only high school in Northern California in the 1970s that had a state-of-the-art computer lab. Furthermore, the school's computer club had a group of parents that were active and willing to raise funds to ensure that their students would continually have access to the latest technology and hardware.

Using this unique and hard-to-find equipment, Bill and his friends were able to repeatedly hack into the University of California's mainframe computer—a task thought unattainable by mere high school students. Emboldened by their continued success, and as an act of teenage bravado, Bill and his friends sought access to higher levels of the university's network. In a deal to keep the kids at bay, the computer administrators at the university granted Bill and his friends unlimited access to their lab in return for an agreement not to breech their system from the outside. The students accepted the offer and spent every waking hour working with some of America's finest computer equipment.

Few would argue that Bill Gates isn't a genius with a once-in-a-generation mind. But his story forces us to ask: Would the behemoth Microsoft exist if Gates had gone to a different high school? Would his insatiable curiosity and intellect have been spent in pursuit of a different passion? Would he have been a doctor, engineer, architect, or lawyer? Was Bill Gates destined for computer greatness—or the recipient of serendipity and opportunity?

I suspect that his unique intellect and tenacity would have proven him successful no matter the avenue he chose to pursue. But perhaps greatness lays in wait for those who can marry opportunity with their talent into the perfect fit. We may never know what would have happened had Mr. and Mrs. Gates, Sr. chosen a house in a different ZIP code, but what stands before us is living proof that extraordinary things can happen when the right person is in the right place at the right time.

* * *

After spending four happy years at Marcos de Niza, I decided to leave teaching. I was suddenly running from plane to plane, sharing my passion for leadership with anyone who would listen. In my own way, I felt as if I had found my fit. I combined my skills and talents with my passion for leadership at a time when there seemed to be a void. I had surrounded myself with people who shared my vision and were willing to help me see it through. I was three years into my new pathway and was finally seeing some success, which only meant more time on planes.

As a part of my nomadic lifestyle, I became used to operating in a sleep-deprived daze, and one early September morning was no different. I was working my way through a crowded gate area to board my plane. Another city, another day, another workshop. The passion of sharing the message of leadership came with of the nightmare of airline travel. As I was standing in line to board, I received a text. It was from David Duarté.

"What are you doing on December seventeenth?"

Running late and having little time to chat, I responded simply with a question mark. Another text followed: "What are you doing on December seventeenth?"

A quick check of my schedule confirmed what I already knew to be true, and I responded with, "Nothing... are you looking to book a workshop?"

They were now making the final call for my flight and I was in full-on travel mode. I boarded the plane, navigated the maze of weary passengers, hoisted my well-organized carry-on into an open bin, sat down, and settled in for a two-hour flight. As I reached to turn off my cell phone, a final text appeared that said, "Not anymore. You're conducting my band at Midwest."

My mind raced with thoughts and admittedly some shock. In fact, I didn't even know he had applied, much less been accepted.

I still get chills thinking about that moment. As a shared dream with almost all who call music education their profession, I had always wanted to conduct on the vaunted stage at the Chicago Hilton. While I had stood there as a performer, and even presented a clinic, I knew those experiences would pale in comparison to the magic of standing in front of an ensemble. I figured that when I left the classroom, this was one of my dreams that would remain unrealized.

When David Duarté left Marcos de Niza, he was done teaching. He was burned out and wanted to never again be a high school band director. Who would have thought that the self-described program killer was really a program creator in waiting? Not David, because when he stopped looking for the perfect fit, the perfect fit went looking for him.

In 1996, an embattled and struggling Apple brought Steve Jobs back as CEO in a last-ditch effort to save the company. Much like Duarté, Jobs had never imagined a time when he would return to the place that had frustrated him so greatly. And just as no one could have seen just how far and how fast Apple would go, the same held true for David Duarté and the Deer Valley High School Band.

* * *

It was a cold December day in the Chicago. The chairs were set, the stage prepped, band tuned, microphones adjusted, and audience in place. As we stood in the Grand Ballroom of the Chicago Hilton and Towers at the Midwest Clinic, I could not have been more amazed or more proud as David kicked off his first number, *The Attack of the Killer Tomatoes*.

Fate has a funny and ironic way of reminding you of things you might otherwise want to forget. As I approached David about the possibility of being a part of this book, he was once again preparing for change. David was in his final hours as a band director and was moving to the District Office to be a Fine Arts Coordinator. As we reminisced about the past and how I had replaced him seven years ago, we both chuckled at the fact that his final act as a band director was to attend a playoff game with his band against our former school, Marcos de Niza. At the end of the game, David's school had lost and Marcos had won. My guess is that fate was somehow exacting payback for what had happened seven years before, when Marcos lost and David's school had won.

Every time I see a Mac versus PC commercial I think of David, playing both characters, still trying to find his fit.

Chapter Three

Sammy the Bull

On creating a culture with Darrin Davis of Broken Arrow High School

Jimmy Moran was my neighbor. We weren't good friends, in fact we weren't even casual acquaintances. We didn't share power tools or exchange lawn care tips. We didn't sit together and hoist a beer while talking sports. In fact, to the best of my knowledge, we never even met. Given his proximity, it is more than likely that we were in the same place at the same time on more than one occasion, but we were never formally introduced. Friends of mine had met him and said he was nice enough, and by all accounts, he was a good man and a fine neighbor. Like so many other people in my neighborhood, community, time, opportunity, or inclination never allowed us to make a connection.

Other than his strong East Coast accent, Jimmy Moran is relatively undistinguishable from everyone else I know. He is an everyday man who neither stands out nor fades away in a crowd. He is skilled in the art of conversation but also knows when not to use it. He is memorable but not remarkable; statuesque but not imposing; strong but not stout; well manicured but not distinguished; reflective but not stoic. He, or someone like him, crosses your path hundreds of times each and every day: in the grocery store, gas station, or standing in line at Starbucks. He is a husband, father, and grandfather and is passionate about his family's success and safety. When asked about family, he said:

"We love each other. We truly care for each other."

Jimmy was my type of guy and lived a Rockwellian portrait of suburban living: two kids, two cars, and a modest home complete with the overprotective dog defending the homestead. The jewelry he wore on his hands indicated success, but the calluses next to them were indications of a life of hard work. Some might say that Jimmy was a remarkably unremarkable person who was living the American dream as a part of the American work force.

As the owner of a successful pool construction business, Jimmy had earned the respect of his coworkers and colleagues. He was squeaky clean, straightforward, and easy to deal with. His background in the steel and concrete industries, coupled with a red-hot construction market in Phoenix, made this business a natural fit for his skill sets.

Despite the strong start and natural draw to the profession, his first venture (pool excavation and concrete substructures) folded after what appeared to be an improbable start. As quickly as the clients appeared, they disappeared. During the initial startup, it seemed he could do no wrong, but soon afterward it seemed that he could suddenly do no right. The business folded after eighteen months, but he was not to be deterred. A man with an entrepreneurial soul and a fighting spirit, he did not stay down for long. Taking a cue from his city's namesake, Phoenix, he would rise from the ashes to succeed again. If other pool construction companies would not use his services, then he would start his own and put them out of business, which is exactly what he did. Creative Pools was born out of necessity and grew out of adversity. It was not long until Jimmy was once again on top and calling the shots.

Most people would find his rise to the top improbable, given the failure of his first business and declining economy, but his ability to accept loss and move on is a trait that others in business might find difficult to cultivate. After investing so much of one's self, personally and professionally, into a new venture, most people find it difficult to move on and start again. As with any significant loss, a period of mourning seems almost natural if not logical. This was not the case with Jimmy.

With the adeptness of a chameleon, he was able to almost instantaneously adjust to his new surroundings and seamlessly move forward with virtually no perceivable adverse effect on either him or his family. He held no fondness for his past nor did he harbor any remorse. The way he saw it, what was done was done.

Clearly, Jimmy Moran was either a person of exceptional spirit or someone extremely adept at change. Had it not been for a twist of fate and a persistent reporter, we might never know that it was both. We might also never have known his real name: Sammy "The Bull" Gravano, an underworld boss who turned federal informant in 1992.

Unless you are a fan of trench-coat thrillers or Harrison Ford movies, you might not know much about the Federal Witness Protection Program. Few people have more than a cursory understanding of how this program operates. WitSec, much like its sister program, the Presidential Protection Detail, simultaneously operates in public and is a highly secretive organization. The Witness Protection Program's mission is to protect highly valued people who have agreed to testify against mob and terror organizations in exchange for a new identity, a relocation package, and around-the-clock protection.

Following the acceptance of a witness into the program, the Marshals Service is tasked with creating a new identity and finding a new culture for the witness, his family, and any endangered associates. This requires the coordination of multiple government agencies, good timing, and total secrecy.

The Witness Protection Program was founded in 1970 in an effort to help the Federal Government protect its most valuable witnesses in the war against organized crime. Those who have witnessed a crime and those who have committed one are treated as equals. The mission: to create, preserve, and foster a new identity and culture for its enrollees. This is a secret society beyond all others and its members neither hold club meetings or participate in community service projects. Their sole objective is to create a new facade for their witnesses that is unlike their past.

Participants are given new names, new identities, assistance with vocational training, and other services as needed. Simply put, a new identity and a new life is created for them from scratch. All of this is done with the idea of creating anonymity by making them indistinguishable from those in their communities. The less they stick out as being different, the less likely they are to be identified under their former identity. They are in big cities and small towns, and are strongly encouraged to become a genuine part of the fabric of their local communities. They are required to be self sufficient and live within their means. They can earn as much or as little as they are capable of, and other than monitoring and protection, are only given assistance during the initial phases of the relocation process. They are encouraged to stay out of the spotlight but not so much as to appear to be seen as avoiding it. They are members of their communities, churches, civic groups, and professional organizations. They may be bankers, small business owners, or even teachers. Teachers like Darrin Davis.

Darrin Davis, if that's his real name, shares some remarkable characteristics with Sammy. His stature is unremarkable but strong. His lack of a perceptible accent and blonde hair points to a history not of Oklahoma. He is seemingly kind and gentle, and yet remarkably strong and resilient. He takes a last-place finish and Grand National Championship in stride and is seen by others as unflappable. In a profession filled with drama and emotion, he is able to shy away from displaying either in public. If there is a mold for music education, Darrin Davis was most certainly not made from it.

Upon first glance, Darrin seems as unlikely a person as any to have come from WitSec. In his community he is well known, well educated, and well liked. He dresses sharply and appreciates the fit and feel of a car not found at your local Ford dealership. He understands hard work and is able to work not only hard, but smart as well. He is equally at home in coach or first class and would just as soon sit down for a plate of pasta among friends as he would share the company of colleagues at a fine resort. He has a strong but quiet presence and wears his heart on his sleeve. He is engaging and charming, and can move throughout the many circles of the music education profession seamlessly and virtually unknown. In this way he is no different than a lot of people, including Sammy Gravano.

Virtually everyone in the Broken Arrow community has heard of Darrin, but few people outside his inner circle truly know him. He is familiar and personal without being too revealing. He is an upstanding man and a pillar in his community. He has spent the majority of his life in this rural city outside of Tulsa, and yet had it not been for the National Championship in 2006, few people outside of his circle of friends and professional colleagues would be able to recognize him in a police lineup.

Darrin has a passion for music and has made it his life's work. As the Director of Bands at Broken Arrow High School he has built a coalition of students, staff, parents, boosters, and community members with the sole focus of ensuring the success of the program and its student members. He is a bright and genial man who is seen as a model teacher, but underneath lurks hints of previous and possibly unfulfilled passions or past experiences in math and/or architecture.

Darrin entered the teaching ranks as quietly as could be as the fifth assistant in a six-teacher program. He assumed that he was safe from infamy and was convinced that no one would pay attention to a junior high band director teaching in a double-wide trailer in a suburb of Tulsa, Oklahoma. He neither sought nor shunned attention. He was content in his place, but as soon as he arrived, was quickly seen as the heir apparent. He was a rising star and did not waste any time in working his way up the ranks of this distinguished and storied program.

It seems unlikely that the WitSec program would place someone in a position or town such as this, but unlikely and unpredictable is what makes the Witness Protection Program so successful. They have been known to slip participants in through side doors with one bodyguard while they parade police cars down Main Street in an attempt to distract and thwart those seeking to silence the witness.

While the WitSec program does not publicly disclose or discuss their operational procedures, Broken Arrow and the education profession could be seen as a logical fit for placement. This sleepy suburb of Tulsa is a bedroom community that places a premium on privacy and respect. People understand that your home is your castle and your work is to be left at work. They would rather talk about the weather than the news, and honor the southern traditions of church and family. Broken Arrow is close to an urban center but far from the prying eyes of a big city, with ample opportunity for employment and housing. Yes, I am speculating, but I would bet that Tulsa and the rest of

Oklahoma is well represented within the enrollment folios of this clandestine program.

To get some perspective, the bands at Broken Arrow High School have been a mainstay of their community and a program of regional and national prominence for decades. Laypeople and community members have long known of the tradition of excellence that is The Pride. Given this, one might think that WitSec would shun such a placement, since participants typically hide from the spotlight. However, the light had been shining on this program for so long that community members took it for granted and saw the program as more of a machine than a program led by a man—and Darrin knew it. Even during my discussion with him, Darrin was quick to point out that The Pride is a collective and communal effort that relies on the synergy of students, staff, parents, and their school community. They make it a point to celebrate their past as much as the present. The bands at Broken Arrow have a rich tradition of excellence dating back to the 1930s and a heritage that they work to keep alive. At a recent band banquet attended by almost seven hundred people, each of the seven living men who have served as the Director of Bands at Broken Arrow were recognized and honored for their contribution to the modern-day Pride. As Darrin is quick to point out, he did not create success at Broken Arrow, but acknowledges that he has helped to elevate it.

The key to fitting in is to be able to balance the need to blend in with your surroundings without being bland. You want to be noticed, but never remembered; and if anyone has done that, Darrin Davis has. Everything about The Pride is distinctive. In all of America they stand as one of the true iconic brands in the marching arts. Few people inside our profession are not aware of The Pride and their distinctive appearance, but even fewer could point out its director, even if he were in a police lineup—assuming that he got caught again. It seems odd that someone so successful could be so unrecognizable. It also seems odd that someone who is trying to fly under the radar has assumed the helm of an organization so widely respected and popular. When you think about it, though, by associating himself with something so large he is dwarfed in comparison. Notoriety is about comparison and perspective. Texas seems big until you compare it to China.

This chapter may seem long until you compare it to a chapter in *War and Peace*. George Clooney gets less attention on the red carpet when he is followed by Brad Pitt. Dwayne Wade was *the* heart and soul of the NBA's Miami Heat until LeBron James made him just another teammate. Perhaps the secret to not being noticed is standing next to someone or something more significant than yourself. By associating himself with something as successful as The Pride, perhaps Darrin is in fact, hiding himself. Brilliant!

Nothing symbolizes this juxtaposition like the name of the Broken Arrow band program. Google *The Pride* combined with *marching band* and over 43,000 hits result. As common as the name seems to be, at Broken Arrow this approach takes on a life of its own. Nothing in this meticulously crafted culture is left to chance. The group has a unique and singular motto, credo, and understanding of purpose. They truly have found a unique approach inside the cultural phenomenon that is high school marching band. By embedding in the program tradition and innovation in equal parts they have created a culture in which students celebrate old-school values in a cutting-edge way. By teaching character through the curricula, process is taught as a part of creating the product. By demanding uniformity in how program members look, uniformity in how they feel is created . Through a delicate balance of music and mission the fulcrum of excellence is found.

If you were to ask someone what makes the BA (as members call themselves) so unique, they might point to their distinctive uniforms or unmistakable musical and marching style. But spend any time at all observing a rehearsal and you'll know that the physical manifestations of the BA uniqueness are just a small portion of what makes the program so special. What you see is what you get; but what you get is not because of what you see. The group's choice of rehearsal and performance uniform is just a small component of the bigger picture.

The marching band world is driven in large part by the visual component of what we as band leaders do, not just on the field, but off the field as well. Beyond the obvious elements of drill and uniform, we have band tee shirts, jackets, banners, trucks, and trophies. Even though most music educators consider music the primary focus of the art form, to the uneducated ear and untrained eye, it is hard to know that by looking at a program. Parents and performers alike seek outward validation of accomplishment and belonging, not just because of what it represents (band), but who they represent (school and community). This sense of belonging is woven into the very fabric of the activity for everyone involved, including spectators. And as with many things in our culture, the greater the successes of the program, the more people emulate and idolize members. This is where Broken Arrow has established an iconic name for itself. Not only is there a strong visual identity both on and off the field, the name is embedded into the hearts, minds, and souls of the entire community. Ask Darrin Davis what sets The Pride apart from its peers and he will tell you that it is the Broken Arrow approach to making music and its unique blend of electronics and wind band sound that sets it apart. Ask any parent or community member and they will immediately talk about the uniform, the name, the drill, the shows, etc. From the inside, it is all music. From the outside, it is all visual. In reality, is a combination of the two.

Darrin says,

> In Broken Arrow, we have a historical museum dedicated to preserving the history of the city. It's hard to believe, but there is an entire section of the museum dedicated just to The Pride. As a part of the display, they have memorabilia, recordings and uniforms from our past. In fact, just the other day, I sent them some of our props from ZO (this year's show). It's humbling to see the display and an honor to know I am a part of the legacy of success here in BA.

Many marching groups have tried to emulate or borrow elements of The Pride in the hopes that it will help them to replicate Broken Arrow's success. They copy the uniform, the schedule, the creed, the logo, and so much more. People have tried to emulate the program's music and drill, and have even adopted the "pre-show" concept that Broken Arrow has become known for. These are important elements of the program's identity, but they are more after effects or byproducts of the culture than the result of it.

It is not what they do, but the manner in which they do it that makes BA culture so enviable and distinct. Every group rehearses, but it is how BA rehearses that sets helps to embed its belief systems without preaching or forcing the issue. It is the way the staff communicates expectations. It is the tone and tenor of rehearsals and the director's ridiculously high expectations. It is their professionalism and profound sense of commitment to student success. It is their wit, warmth, and wisdom. It is their ability to use each other's strengths to cover their weaknesses—and none of this can be worn on a jacket or embossed on a tee shirt.

When I asked Darrin to define the culture at Broken Arrow, he struggled to put it into words.

> Trying to define our culture is challenging, because it's not any one single thing, it's a culmination of what we do every day. We want the kids to be the same person outside of rehearsal as they are during rehearsal, so we practice our culture while we are practicing our music. The

culture of our program has evolved over such a long period of time it is hard to know what I can truly take credit for and what was here prior to my arrival. The line between my life here as a student, assistant director, and now director has been blurred by so many incredible experiences that I can hardly delineate between them.

For instance, the kids are expected to respond to instruction with a YES SIR. We did that when I was in band and it has carried forward. It's not something we ask the students to do, just something they expect of themselves. A lot of things have evolved that way.

The same thing happened with our rehearsal dress code. For one rehearsal we asked the kids one day to wear white tee shirts and khaki shorts so we could clean a particularly hard drill move. After that, the kids just sort of took it on as a part of their culture. After awhile, they created "crazy sock day," still wearing the rehearsal uniform, but making it their own, a little more personal.

"As the architect of the organization, surely you must have some blueprint for the process?" I asked. Darrin paused, almost as if to ensure he was not going to say something he shouldn't or tip his hand on something we shouldn't know.

It starts with the education of the students, not just their music education but their character education as well. We stress from day one that they are a part of something larger than just themselves. We remind them of the successes and sacrifices that have been made to get the program to this point and that it is to be respected and honored.

I reminded Darrin that education and indoctrination are separated by a very fine line, much as are the labels crazy and genius. He smiled wryly, implying he knew exactly what I was saying yet acknowledged nothing.

It's not what you do, it's what you don't do… you know? It's the little things. The things you wouldn't find in a manual or a rule book.

I pushed him for an example. Darrin says,

I make the boys cut their hair every year.

Infringing on their personal appearance creates a certain amount of conflict, but deep down inside they like it. If we are clean-cut people, we will act in a clean-cut way. We are in the Bible belt and there is not a major metropolitan city within four hours. Our culture is a product of our community. Our core values aren't just ours; they are our community's core values.

We talk about history and heritage a lot and we are serious about educating the students about it. In fact, if we have an infraction against our code and a punishment is required, often it's trophy cleaning duty. We believe that everyone who enters the band room, student and adults alike, should know where we have been and what we have done. Our history is on display for all to see and set up in chronological order. Honestly, most of the time a member receives this punishment, they enjoy doing it.

Educating our students about our history and culture is an ongoing process, with many character elements, but the keyword we keep coming back to is *integrity*. Every day we pull everyone in and we talk about something related to it. It's not a scripted spiel, but an honest dialogue about who we are and what we are trying to achieve. Honestly, even though the bulk of our time with the band is spent pursuing musical and visual excellence, we address character and heritage on some level every day. We do this with our students and we do this with our staff as well. They understand that if it is going to work, it has to start with them.

We do the same thing with the parents. Each year, we have an orientation meeting in which we not only discuss the rules and regulations but the values as well. We have a program for the returning parents to adopt a new member and their family. Before each show the vet parents do something special for their adoptee. They also serve as a support network and band guidance counselor for that first year. They are there to celebrate and support that family when they have a question, concern, or are in need of information. We try to assign the adoptive parents a new member that is outside of their child's section and circle of friends. In this way we create and accelerate the bonding process for the child and the parents.

Anyone who understands the stranglehold that organized crime has on certain industries will tell you that their power comes from two things: their strength of conviction and the fact that they are loyal to a fault.

Whether instilled by fear or respect, a member of the mob is a made man for life, regardless how long or short that life is. In fact, until Sammy Gravano turned on John Gotti, no high ranking member of organized crime had ever served as a state's witness against another member of the Mafia. As a result of Gravano's testimony, not only did John Gotti go to jail, but it weakened the entire East Coast mob organization.

Darrin understands the strength of moving in a pack. It is more than a part of The Pride creed; it is a philosophy embedded into everyday rehearsals and performances.

Everywhere we move, we move together in a block. The kids silently walk arm in arm, and in lockstep as we move from place to place. The intensity is palpable both within and outside of the ranks and is an impressive sight to see. Honestly, even after all these years here, I still get goose bumps when I see it and it is one of my favorite moments of the year. In addition to being an organized way for us to get from place to place, it also allows the students the time and opportunity to mentally prepare for what they are about to do. As a staff, we ask the group to move as a group when in public, but how they chose to move as a group evolved from the students.

We are constantly stressing that when we perform, we mean business. We prepare to do something and then we expect students to do it. They have an obligation not just to their peers but to themselves to be the very best they can be.

When young people try to max out for a performance or competition, they are far more likely to make a mistake. To fail to achieve what you are capable of is a failure on a personal and organizational level.

We stress confidence and control. We want every student we work with to know that they are expected to operate at the highest level possible but not to try and overreach. The ability to operate at your maximum potential is what is expected, not just by the staff, but by the students as well.

While many organizations seek to replicate the Broken Arrow program's unique sense of oneness and ability to stand out within the crowded field of high school marching bands, few programs have succeeded. There is a strong sense of identity and loyalty associated with The Pride that is palpable from the moment you step into their well worn and dated band room. Whether you see them in performance or in their pre-performance block, their gait and gaze are haunting and unforgettable. This is not something that a normal fourteen-year-old does with comfort and ease. This is something that is trained and infused into them by the program, presumably by a seasoned pro or someone who has been through the process of creating an identity before.

The similarities between The Pride and the Mob are both alarming and interesting. Just like the Mob, members of The Pride are not secretive about how they go about their business. They are forthright and confident about who they are, and anyone else's inability to stop them from achieving their objectives. They are family, friends, and formidable foes. They have a singular sense of purpose and have little concern for how it is seen by others. They are there to not only stretch themselves but to stretch the boundaries of what's possible. In fact, one of The Pride's core values is, "To do what's never been done." They are as close to a cultural phenomenon as there is in the music education profession, and they leave outsiders wondering not only how BA does it but asking if can it be replicated. Broken Arrow's unique stature among America's elite music organizations has been the subject of many back room conversations, blog postings, newspaper articles, trade journal segments, and even an award-winning documentary. While Sammy has appeared on *60 Minutes*, even he doesn't have a full-length documentary.

> Maintaining the culture is one of the hardest parts of the job. Like any group, you have to change with the times and circumstances. The Pride is no different. The program at Broken Arrow is actually separated into three high school campuses, with two campuses housing ninth and tenth grades and one senior high campus housing eleventh and twelfth grades. In the early 1990s we had two separate marching bands at the intermediate high schools and one marching band at the senior high school, but we felt that was limiting the organization's growth and unity. We also required every student to participate in the marching band. Not only did the physical separation divide our staff and resources, but it created a separation and competition among students who would one day all be in the same band. We decided that this was not meeting the needs of the organization

and decided to make a change. We eliminated the two intermediate marching bands, opened The Pride up to everyone from ninth through twelfth grades, and made it voluntary.

Once we decided to move forward with this new format, we needed a way to remind the kids that regardless of which school they attended, they now needed to walk, talk, and play like one, so one of our staff members, Michael Raiber, adapted a poem from The Jungle Book and made it our creed.

> Now here is the creed of The Pride;
> it's true and blue as the sky.
> All who believe it shall prosper,
> and those who deny it pass by.
> Upon this field of dreams
> we all receive our due,
> for this is the place where they all come true.
> As with all things most important,
> it's where our hearts and souls abide.
> For the strength of The Pride is the member,
> and the strength of the member is The Pride.

At first, the band didn't understand why we were doing this, but we got the student leaders to buy in and let them present it to the rest of the group, and within a month, it caught fire. Now, it is a part of the fabric of our group.

Today, the word *Mafia* is used to refer to almost any organized crime group, and in some cases is even used to describe groups completely unrelated to crime. In organized crime there is a hierarchy, with higher ranking members making decisions that trickle down to the other members of the Family. The Mafia is not a single group or gang; it is made up of many families that sometimes fight each other, and sometimes cooperate in the interest of achieving greater power or control. Members of competing families occasionally even agree to serve on a commission that makes major decisions affecting all of the Mob families. Most of the time, though, they simply consent to stay out of each other's way with the understanding that others will do the same.

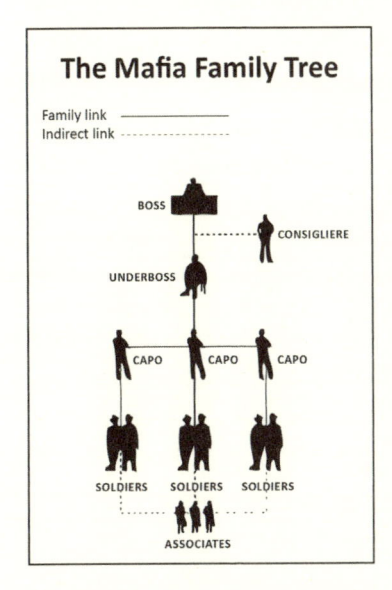

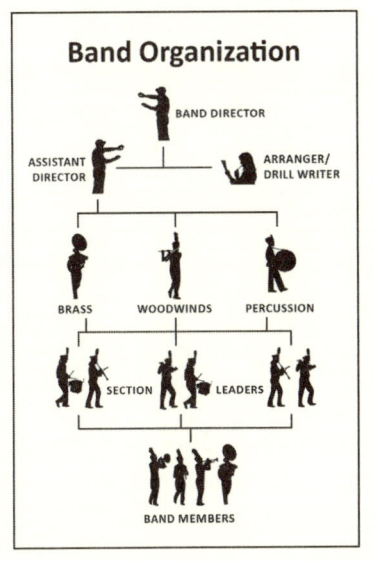

The Mafia Family Tree

Family link ———
Indirect link --------

BOSS
CONSIGLIERE
UNDERBOSS
CAPO CAPO CAPO
SOLDIERS SOLDIERS SOLDIERS
ASSOCIATES

Band Organization

BAND DIRECTOR
ASSISTANT DIRECTOR
ARRANGER/ DRILL WRITER
BRASS WOODWINDS PERCUSSION
SECTION LEADERS
BAND MEMBERS

In this way, The Pride, and marching bands all across America, are not much different. Both groups have a defined hierarchy and structure. In the Mafia, this is well understood and adhered to strictly. The lowest levels of the organization are called *Soldiers*. They are supervised by mid-level associates called *Capos*. The next rung up the ladder is the coveted spot of *Underboss*. The Underboss is someone who enjoys many of the financial benefits and power associated with the family Don, who is simply called the *Boss*. There are outside associates who serve in an advisory capacity to the bosses called *Consigliere*.

In much the same way, marching band members are supervised by student leaders, who report to the caption heads, who report to the assistant director, who reports to the head director. The director typically acts in an autocratic fashion, but seeks outside counsel, help, and advice from the *Consiglieres* of our profession (drill writers, choreographers, guest conductors, adjudicators, and so on).

At first glance, one might blanch at our educational art form being compared to such a disreputable organization. However, directors young and old have been called much worse as they pursue perfection through musical discipline and visual conformity. What makes The Pride different from others is their level of success at doing just that. What makes the Mafia different from any other gang is the same: their ability to demand and enforce complete discipline and conformity.

Members of both marching bands and the Mafia understand that safety and success comes from sacrifice and willingness to commit to something larger than oneself. Anyone who has ever worked with or participated in a marching band understands this all too well. There is a direct and corollary relationship between sacrifice and success. The more you are willing to sacrifice, the more likely you are to find success. To each individual, the balance of the success they pursue and the sacrifice required to achieve it is a delicate and ongoing process. To be a part of The Pride you not only sacrifice your time, sweat, and tears, but also some of your personal identity. When you join The Pride, you make a commitment to the 240 other people who count on you for *their* success, and in that way, you also commit yourself to their success and their expectations as well.

In The Pride there is a silent code of behavior borne through peer-to-peer modeling. It begins with the staff and their unrelenting commitment to the rehearsal process, but in the end, it falls to the students to adapt and respond, both individually and collectively. This on-the-job training is swift, strong, unforgiving, and on display for everyone to see at each and every rehearsal. From student led pre-rehearsal stretches to after-rehearsal sectionals, it is clear that students have accepted and embraced their call to arms and are not afraid to hold their peers accountable. This culture was established by the Broken Arrow directors, but is enforced by the members. They are committed to the process, but more importantly to the people involved in it, adult and student alike. They are loyal to each other and loyal to the cause.

Darrin was reminded of this lesson through recent tragic events. When his mother passed away unexpectedly in December of 2008, his world was shaken. The Pride knew his mother well as an active band booster and surrogate mother. A loss for Darrin meant a loss to The Pride, and when one suffers, they all suffer, adults included.

After my mother passed, the organization went to work and the result was nothing short of amazing. The staff and students took over and did whatever it took to make sure that I could focus on my family and not my job. My mother lived for The Pride, and in her passing The Pride helped me to keep on living for my mother. The culture was who my mother was, and after she was gone, the support was like nothing I had ever experienced. Even to this day, it blows my mind.

In the case of Broken Arrow, it is hard to tell which came first, the chicken or the egg. Did success of The Pride come from the organizational structure, or did the organizational come from success?

"Perhaps a little bit of both," Darrin says with a knowing smirk. He pauses and continues, "but if I had to choose one over the other, I would choose the structure, as I think it can help to produce success."

For example:

> It was the run up to the 2007 Grand Nationals and we just weren't getting the impact or scores we wanted from the visual end of the program. The staff discussed it and we came to the conclusion that the design of the uniform and the complexity of the drill were overbearing to

the visual production. We felt that if we could simplify the uniform a little it would go a long way toward presenting the demand of the drill in a more simplified fashion.

For those who have not seen The Pride, their look is as timeless as it is groundbreaking. Traditional rules of black pants and dark lines were ignored in favor of a highly stylized and aggressive design that presents as many challenges as it does opportunities. The all black-and-white uniform has a split-color left leg that presents a high degree of exposure for foot timing and design issues when students are marching in different directions. The design is completed by a fourteen-inch white plume on top and a left shoe that is half black and half white. There are many who questioned it, and even more that admire it, but to be sure, when you ask people about The Pride, the uniform is usually the first thing they talk about.

The decision to make the switch back to the more traditional pants was not a decision made lightly. We deliberated for a long time, but in the end, the staff felt that the complexity of the show had evolved past the uniform. The staff knew the kids would be upset, but even I was surprised by the reaction of our members. I sat the group down before rehearsal one day and shared with them our decision and the rationale for it. As soon as the words left my lips, you could see the disappointment in their eyes. At first, the students felt as if they had failed in some way. But failure turned to anger quickly, as if I had taken something away from them. They felt that their identity had been compromised. I was shocked by their response and by the deepness of their resentment. The members saw the uniform as their tradition and the sole source of their uniqueness—and they could not have been more wrong.

I have to tell you that it takes a lot to get me angry, but their response had pushed me to that point. After all that we had done together, it seemed as if the students didn't trust or believe that the staff was making a decision that was in their best interest. The members didn't see that we were trying to evolve forward, but saw it as a step backward. Over and over, the staff kept hearing the word "tradition" from the kids.

Tradition is a word you hear a lot in music education, and while it is important for maintaining some form of continuity, it should never inhibit your educational objectives. Tradition is a way for people to hold on to what is familiar. We had to take the time to explain to the students that their identity was not in the color of their pants, but in the young people wearing them. They were told, "We are not a fashion statement; we are an organization in pursuit of musical excellence and character development." The Pride of Broken Arrow was this way before these uniforms and will be long after the uniforms are gone. While we may be remembered for what we look like, we are not defined by it.

I guess I could have and should have seen that coming. After all, teens are so wrapped up in how they look and how they can stand out, rather than finding out who they are and where they fit best. I just didn't make that correlation. These students are so mature and insightful that I sometimes forget that they are still teenagers. We ended up allowing them to wear their "colors" during the awards presentation, which helped unruffle their feathers.

The marching art form is broken up into musical and visual responsibilities, which all too often lead people to try to establish their identities in these areas. You hear, "we always do jazz," or, "our show tells a story," or, "we are more of a concert band program," when in fact, it is not what you do but how you do it that has the most impact on your culture. It is not the color of your uniforms, the notes on the page, or the story you are sharing which defines you; it is how you wear it, the way you rehearse it, and the reason you are sharing the story that tells us who you are.

Darrin says,

> Culture is more of an abstract concept, whereas traditions are more concrete. People often intermingle the two because it makes it more definable, concrete, and understandable.
>
> Our students come from three different campuses with significant differences in backgrounds, affluence, and musical skill sets. Our band rooms are dilapidated portables, and until this past year, our performance hall was the gymnasium or local church, whichever would could find the space. But when the students walk through the band room doors, our expectations are that they behave, march, and play in a world-class fashion. We surround and immerse our students in a culture of high standards and significant challenges, which is one of the reasons we participate in Grand Nationals annually. Some people participate to win. We participate to expose our students to the highest standards, the best adjudicators, and the greatest challenges. We are blessed to have wonderful bands in our areas and believe as a staff that as our competitors get better, so do we. To have the privilege of competing on a national level is not something we take for granted and is something we talk about a lot with our students.

Darrin told me,

> I guess our reason for wanting to be on the national stage was said best by you (Scott), after we won Grand Nationals. You said in a letter to the kids: "Perfection may impress, but magic inspires. And given the two, I will always take inspiration. Tonight, I saw magic. Tonight, I was inspired."
>
> In success and in failure we want to inspire. We want to inspire our students, our community, and those involved in the art form of marching. This is not just a performance goal but a daily pathway. Failure is something we choose to not only acknowledge but even celebrate. As a group and as teachers, we have had our share of successes and failures, and although the successes far outnumber the failures, we try to embrace them equally. We believe that our failure to qualify for finals in 2005 was the gateway to our National Championship in 2006. Our failure and disappointment fueled us and pushed us harder than ever before. It was a time of hurt, and we learned the hard way that we were not invincible or as good as we thought we were. These moments were teaching opportunities not to be missed or diminished. We do not shy away from them and we do not regret them. In

order to learn and grow from them, you have to celebrate them. Failure is a source of growth for everyone, student, staff, and parents.

And in that moment, you can almost see the parallel path Darrin was taking. You almost feel that he was not just talking about the group's past, but perhaps his own. Everyone I know says that Darrin Davis is about the nicest, most down-to-earth person you could ever want to meet. They marvel at how someone who is so successful could be so humble. They say that if you did not know who he was, you would never know what he has done with his life. But then again, they said the same thing about Jimmy Moran.

Chapter Four

A Pe-King Duck Out of Water

On connecting with your community with Michael Boitz of Saratoga High School

Driving into the Saratoga High School parking lot for the first time, it was clear that this new home of sunny skies and Asian culture was going to be a radical departure from everything he once knew. As a twenty-something Midwestern boy of Norwegian ancestry, anyone with 20/100 vision could see that he wasn't from around here. His nondescript 1980-something Buick sedan pulling a U-Haul trailer did little to help camouflage his status. And if somehow that were to escape your attention, his thick northern drawl, red hair, freckles, and sun deprived complexion was sure to do the trick.

"We're not in Kansas anymore," he thought to himself.

As soon as he stepped from his rust-encrusted car, placed his feet on the sun-soaked green grass, and smelled the salt air, he knew that his life was about to change. Gone were Minnesota's frigid winters and conservative mindset.

What stood before him were the blue skies and progressive culture of the Silicon Valley suburb he now called home.

For his entire life, Michael Boitz had only known one place. He was born, raised, and college educated in Minnesota. The significant change of scenery and landscape was both physically and emotionally cleansing. Despite the counsel and advice of his friends, he had followed his gut, better judgment, and stubborn father's advice to the small suburban village of Saratoga, located in the epicenter of the tech industry.

Michael's first stop should have been a place where he could shower away the grime of the seventeen-hundred-mile journey, but for the moment, that would have to wait. He drove straight to Saratoga High School, ready to assume what was left of this once proud program. Not wanting to waste a single moment, he walked into the front office, reintroduced himself to the secretarial staff, and asked for his keys and class rosters. With every step he took toward the music hall he now called home, his sense of anticipation and angst grew.

As he walked toward his new classroom, he read through the names on his roster. It seemed almost surreal. His classes, once filled with the children of farmers and day laborers named Johnson, Anderson, and Smith, would now come from the hi-tech, fast-paced culture of Silicon Valley. The names on the list were more akin to a game of Word Jumble than it was a roll sheet.

Michael remembers thinking, "How can I memorize names I can't even pronounce?" He was simultaneously comforted by his belief that all students are the same and terrified by the unknown of his new surroundings. He had made the leap. He had left everything he had known for a place where status was displayed not through your pickup truck and gun rack, but your personal computer and cell phone. As he grew closer to the band room door his uneasiness was somewhat relieved as he saw a hand-painted sign that read:

WELCOME MR. BOITZ, WE'RE GLAD YOU ARE HERE!

There it was, in writing for all the world to see. They had claimed him. There was no turning back. For better or worse, he was theirs, and they were his. You might think that he would have come to grips with these issues during the interview, contract signing, or moving process, but he hadn't. What had escaped him for weeks was now staring him in the face. It was hard to believe that after all he had been through, it was a two-foot by three-foot piece of paper that was paralyzing him with fear. He was suddenly and unexpectedly overwhelmed as the enormity of the challenge washed over him. The poster was as much a premonition as it was paralytic.

> I had never intended to teach at Saratoga High School. Six months earlier, in the midst of the Midwest Clinic, I struck up a conversation with the man next to me at the bar. Unbeknownst to me, this person just happened to be the Music

Supervisor for the Mountain View school district, located in a San Francisco suburb. After rambling on and sharing our thoughts on the clinics and the state of music education, he told me that there were two openings in his district and said he would like to see my name on the list of applicants. I was both shocked and intrigued with the opportunity and made it a point to do some research after returning home.

Three months later, I found myself in northern California on a four day job-hunting junket which by day three had already resulted in three interviews, two offers, and still one more interview to go. Life was good!

I spent the last part of this third day on the beach with friends basking in the glow of my success. As I watched the sunset over the ocean I kept replaying the events of the past few days in my mind. I knew that I had a momentous decision in front of me and started to create mental checklists. I sat there in the sun and reviewed the overwhelming amount of information I needed to process before making a decision about which job to accept. Keep in mind, I had been happy, in fact very happy, in Minnesota and I liked my opportunities there. But this... well, this just felt right. As the waves slowly began to creep toward me and the sun dipped below the horizon, I started thinking out loud about the pros and cons of the two jobs when I realized that I still had one more interview in the morning. My last interview before returning home was at the namesake high school in the hideaway village of Saratoga.

The moment was perfect and I had a lot to be happy about. After two full days of interviews in front of administrators and band boosters, I was excited but I also felt a little bit like the Beverly Hillbillies. I didn't have a pickup truck or hound dog, but the premise was pretty much the same.

Michael had struck gold and was mentally packing up to make the trip out west. The interview scheduled for the next day at Saratoga, a much smaller school, was an afterthought and wasn't on his radar. After all, as he understood it, this was a program that was in a state of disrepair and whose best days had long since passed. With not one but two birds in the hand and the dreary reputation of the Saratoga Music department, he saw no need to venture further into the bush. Michael had come to a decision and it felt good. He shared with the friend who had accompanied him on the trip, Brian Asuma, that he was soon to be the Assistant Director of Bands at Mountain View High School or one of the other two schools that had offered him a job, and was going to cancel tomorrow's interview.

At one o'clock that morning, while winding down after a long day, his friend Brian said, "I think you should go to that Saratoga interview."

Michael balked and said, "Why? It's a rundown program with no one in it."

Brian responded decisively and with authority, "You are going. And just to make sure, I'm going to drive you."

Chalking it up to alcohol induced bravado, he laughed it off and prepared to call it a night. He was in no mood to argue and saw no harm in acquiescing. As they drove back to their hotel he sat in silence and thought, "Why waste my time and theirs?"

Michael awoke the next morning, feeling some aftereffects from a night of revelry and was convinced that his friend Brian, who was feeling similar symptoms, would reconsider his late-night stance, if he even remembered it.

Just then, Brian barged into the room and said, "Up and at 'em sunshine, we have places to go and people to meet."

Michael knew in an instant that there was no getting out of this one.

> The interview was like no other. The panel consisted of eleven people, a group, incidentally, larger than the orchestra program that was a part of the job. A little hung over and slightly unprepared for the overwhelming panel, I started to panic. I tried to stay focused by looking into the eyes of then Principal Kevin Skelly. I was

hoping that by ignoring the rest of the room, I might make them magically disappear. I had used this technique as a refuge before, and for me, it worked. So there I sat, ignoring ten of the eleven people in the room, just counting the minutes until this torturous exercise would be over.

As short questions turned into long conversations and a brief interview passed into three hours, Michael's memory of the process is vague, but he remembers one man with great clarity—the Principal. He knew from those three hours that this was a man of vision and someone he could follow. With each passing moment, Michael felt a connection beginning to grow.

Michael is a people person through and through, and this was what he sought most in his search for work: a connection with someone and something he could identify with. As the marathon interview came to a close and Michael was preparing to leave, Principal Skelly asked him if he had any questions. At first, seeking to terminate this marathon event, he declined. He stood, and extended his hand of gratitude to each of the panel members, and prepared to make his way to the woebegone friend in the school parking lot. After all, Brian had been waiting for over three hours. As he reached for the office door, just steps away from the clean getaway he so wanted, Michael's conscience and curiosity forced a response.

"What do you want from your music program?"

The question seemed perfectly reasonable. In fact, it is almost standard in these types of situations, but as the words left his lips he could feel their importance growing. How could it be that he actually cared enough to ask? How could he, after three long hours, even have a need to ask a question? Was it possible that this afterthought of a program had piqued his interest?

The pause was palpable.

Dr. Skelly said, "We have all of the academic accolades we could ask for. We even have some pretty good athletic programs, but what I want from my music department is a soul. This school has none. A soul... that's what I want from my music program."
"At that moment I was hooked. With that response, I knew that the other jobs I had been offered were a distant second to Saratoga. I wanted this job more than anything."
He was prepared to leave small-town, conservative, white America, a place where he should have felt comfortable, for a job in a community that was more like a foreign country, where he could never be truly comfortable. Michael left Saratoga High School and California with more questions than he came with and no offer from the job he now wanted most. He was now forced to sit, wait, and hope.
Michael returned home with two offers, and yet he was ashamed and embarrassed that the thing he pursued with such mediocrity had now become his first choice. As soon

as the wheels of the plane touched the ground, he began to gather his thoughts and his things. Even with so much to do, unpacking would have to wait. Bags in hand and a suntan on his face, he headed straight to the hospital to be with his ailing father. As soon as he walked through the hospital doors he began to struggle with how much to share. While he wanted to come clean on the events of the past week, the shame of being so woefully unprepared for his final interview would be hard to explain to the working man who had raised him. Michael's father was a person who embodied the values and work ethic of the Midwest. This would not be something that he would look kindly upon, and Michael knew it.

As he entered the room, Michael's fears began to melt at the relief of seeing his father's condition unchanged. After exchanging hugs and a period small talk, the difficult conversation about his trip began. Just as Michael reached the point where he would share his experiences from the final day, the phone rang. It was the call from Principal Skelly.

> I still remember that phone call. I vividly remember standing at my father's hospital bed, trying to appear calm while inside I was exploding with joy. I remember faltering with my words as I accepted the offer. I remember the smell of antiseptic and sick people that permeated the air around me. I remember the elation I felt at receiving the offer, but most of all, I remember the surreal nature of feeling so good while my

father lay in such a fragile state. I knew that my new path would lead me far away from my father at a time when he needed me to be close, but also knew that this was the right thing to do. I was elated not only with the outcome but with the opportunity I had to share that moment with the person who meant the most to me, my father.

It was official. He was the new band and orchestra director at Saratoga High School, which sounded more prestigious than it actually was. He was in charge of reviving this once proud but currently fragile program that by all indications was just a heartbeat away from death. The remainder of his time in Minnesota flew by. The transition of closing up one home and preparing to start another made his days seem short and his to-do list long. Before he knew it, he was back in California, but this time for good. He didn't know where to start. The room was a disaster and had not been updated since Proposition 13 passed in the late 1970s. The instrument inventory was bleak and desperately in need of an overhaul. The entire roster of students could fit on one eight-and-a-half by eleven sheet of paper. The phrase, "Be careful what you wish for, because you just might get it," reverberated through his mind.

"I remember questioning my decision and wondering if I had made an emotional decision instead of a logical one. After all, the program was in shambles and it was clear from the get-go that I was going to have trouble relating to a culture that was so foreign to me."

Michael thought it best to start with the kids.

"I thought... kids are kids. How different can they be?"

He was about to find out. Where he had come from, recruiting was not something you did; kids just wanted to be in band. Recruiting in Minnesota meant that you opened the doors and in the students walked, instrument in hand with at least some cursory knowledge as to who John Phillip Sousa was. Where he came from, they spoke English and their names were something you could pronounce without a degree in a foreign language. He had spent his entire life in Minnesota, a place where practice rooms were not a refuge for old peanut butter and jelly sandwiches, but a place to hone your skills and perfect your craft. And most certainly, orchestra classes were not comprised of six violins, two violas, and one cello.

"This is nothing like Minnesota," I thought. "Heck, I wasn't even sure I was still in America," Michael says with some guilt.

Gone was the excitement of a new locale and the challenges associated with it. The reality was starting to set in and he began to wonder if he had made the right choice.

"What the hell do I do now?"

He did what every Midwestern boy did when they had a problem: he called his dad for advice. He explained the state of the program in painstaking detail, being sure to pontificate on all of his misgivings, trying to paint as bleak a picture as possible.

Years later, I realized that during that conversation I wasn't looking for advice so much as I was looking for permission to quit. After all, I was a successful teacher. I had a master's degree from Northwestern University and had studied with *the* Mallory Thompson. Surely, someone of my stature was worthy of something better than this. Almost as soon as the words left my mouth, I knew that I was lying, and I'm pretty sure my dad knew, too. The truth was, I was scared and didn't know what to do. I wanted to run and hide, but my conscience wouldn't allow it, so I reached out to my father for permission.

As soon as he finished his overtly pessimistic diatribe, there was an uncomfortable silence, after which his father said, "I understand Michael, and I don't blame you for being scared. I love you unconditionally and will be proud of you regardless of the fact you are a chicken s#!t."

He was shocked to hear those words from his father's mouth.

"Did my father just call me that?" he thought. "Could the man who was both educated and eloquent find no other way to describe me? Really?"

His father's word choice and blunt assessment made him angry, and to prove the point, he ended the conversation abruptly. For days Michael could think of nothing else. His father's simultaneous love and disapproval was what drove him to rise in the morning and work through the night.

"I will show him," he thought. "Call me a chicken s#!t? We'll see who the real chicken s#!t is."

Selling kids on music had never been hard for Michael. It was something he was passionate about and believed in with every fiber of his being. His philosophy of "music education for *every* child" included ones whose names he could not pronounce. So he set to work. He spent countless hours on the phone, connecting with each and every student on that single piece of paper. He smiled through it all, misdialing phone numbers and mispronouncing names, but his welcome-to-reality moment came one morning shortly before the start of band camp when a parent showed up at the band room door.

As Michael greeted them and introduced himself, the parent, startled by his youthful appearance said, "You teacher? I no can tell. To me, all Caucasians look the same."

He reached out to anyone and everyone who would listen in the only way he knew how: he listened more than he spoke. He connected with each person on a level that was comfortable not to him, but to them. He ate their food. He visited their homes. He learned their social customs. By connecting with them, he became one of them.

> You have to understand that music is a significant part of the Asian culture. By speaking music, you are speaking their language without speaking their vocabulary. It wasn't hard to convince the students and their parents of the importance of music, just the importance of them taking it

at school. The parents appreciated the sense of culture and discipline that comes with music, but made it clear that it took time away from more important studies. This was something I wasn't used to. At other schools parents fight with kids to join band. At Saratoga, the kids had to fight their parents to join band. Add to that the difficulty in explaining the concept of marching band to someone who had never seen one and you can imagine some of the looks I got. Orchestra was an easier sell, as it was something they understood, but still not a slam-dunk.

The Asian-American culture places a premium on achievement like SAT scores, and class rank as being uber-important. The philosophy of core academic-only education was as foreign to me as their language. I tried to explain the benefits of music and its direct effect on scholastic achievement. I didn't do it because I believed it to be of primary importance, I did it because that was what was important to the parents.

I know that music kids are the most hardworking and enduring kids in school, and I needed to share that with them. After many phone calls and home visits, I learned that they also needed to share some things with me about what they believed. It was a long and slow process that took a great deal of stamina and patient listening. I quickly figured out that I didn't need to change the parents' minds; I just needed to listen to their concerns. The parents did not need to be convinced so much as they needed to be heard.

All the while, call after call, meal after meal, parent meeting after parent meeting, Michael kept reflecting back to his father calling him a chicken s#!t. Although his father would pass away soon afterward, those words would prove to be life altering.

Thirteen years have passed since his father made that comment. Thirteen long years Michael has spent as the music maestro of not only of the high school but the City of Saratoga as well. During that time, the school music program has ballooned to over 400 students in a school of just 1300 kids. The once feeble marching band of fifty students has become an innovative and progressive organization with over 220 participants, and the nonet that once passed for an orchestra has swelled to 120 participants and two full orchestra classes that can play the grand classics with technical proficiency and artistry. As an added bonus, Michael has helped to conceive and bring to fruition a state-of-the-art, multimillion-dollar performing arts facility that stands as an equal of any community hall in the country.

Michael often reflects on those early years both privately and with his students as a way of reminding them how much has changed and how far they have come. While it seems an eternity to those who weren't there, it feels like yesterday to Michael. Yes, the Saratoga music program has changed, but Michael has not. He is still the same Midwestern boy with his impish grin, Opie Taylor looks, and work ethic that built the program. So much has changed, yet so much has remained the same. Michael still works just as hard if not harder than he did in the early days, but he works differently. Where years ago it was about building and convincing the community of the value of music, now he spends his time studying scores, helping to prepare students' college auditions, and every once in awhile, he still grabs a kid in the hallway and asks them how come they're not in music. Yes, the Midwestern work ethic is still there, but the brown Buick is gone and in its place is a slowly deteriorating 1990-something Mustang convertible. His transformation from country to Cali is complete, and through it all he has maintained the best of both worlds.

Despite his smaller stature, you can always spot Michael in a crowd. Just look for the crowd, and there he is. He is not there as a part of the crowd; the crowd is there as a part of him. "Boitz," as his students call him, is not a kid magnet so much as he is a people magnet. His energy is endless and his enthusiasm is boundless. He gesticulates wildly with virtually every sentence and could disarm a small militia with his smile. Whether he is reading his group the riot act or reading a menu, he can command a room and is a polished public speaker. A friend to all and a foe to none, Michael truly is someone who can connect on an earnest level with anyone in his path.

Michael is now the Department Chair and general pied piper for all things melodious in Saratoga. Beyond being connected to his students and his community, he is connected to his profession. He is a member of CMEA, MENC, the Bay Section of CMEA, CBDA, CODA, ASTA, WBA, NCBA, IAJE, CTEA, and the NEA. His list of affiliations and titles reads like a bowl of alphabet soup instead of a business card. Just for good measure, he is also a Rotarian and swears that he is the only one at meetings who isn't already collecting Social Security. He believes that as time consuming as they are, the demands of being so embedded in activities outside of school don't take away from success; they ensure it.

> Connecting with people takes time and effort. There were a lot of times after a long day of teaching that I just wanted to go home, but I didn't. I went to meetings, communal gatherings, socials events and everything else I was invited to. To an even greater extent, you have to keep in mind that I eat and shop in the same community where I work. In some respects, the job is always right there in my face. It took me a long time to be okay with that, for it to be healthy.

When you see the chameleon-like skills of Michael and the personal and professional success it has brought, it begs the question: How connected are we as music educators?

In our school history classes we were taught the concept of *laissez-faire*, the French political doctrine commonly known as "hands off." Following its European roots, the term literally means, "let do." The concept is simple. What is your problem is your problem, and my involvement will help neither you nor me. This philosophy is often used to describe isolationists, protectionists, and people who generally believe that the less we worry about each other and the more we worry about ourselves, the better off we will be. Once a highly valued and popular economic and political mantra, it is getting harder with each passing day to argue the merits of it in today's interconnected society.

The oceans that surround us no longer separate us. The airspace that surrounds us is easily navigable to all, and to a handful of nations, so are the heavens above. To an even greater extent, the blue skies filled with silent, streaming bits of information from all corners of the world are just as dangerous as the weapon systems on the ground. Truly, there are few places in today's world where one can hide from advancing technology and global connectivity. It is hard to deny that our world is getting smaller, and few could credibly assert that laissez-faire is a realistic way to deal with the complex problems we face. If nothing else, the tragic events of 9/11 have taught us that peace in America starts and ends with peace on earth.

What is true for the world at large is true for the world of music education. The difference is that, unlike the rest of the world, we as music educators have not learned the same lessons. Like our world, the profession of music education is facing challenges that are ever increasing and that place our very existence in peril. Our generation of music educators has been witness to something akin to a professional and educational genocide. All across our country the alarm bells are ringing and programs are disappearing while we wait for someone else to stand up and say "Enough!" We are a profession under siege, and rather than stand united and face our challenges, we stand divided in hopes that they do not come for us. We are the professional embodiment of laissez-faire.

Ask yourself: If/when the principal cuts the choral program, will I stand and fight? When the district enforced new scheduling restrictions on your elementary schools, what did you do? Did you schedule a meeting with those in power? Did you send a well-crafted memo detailing the long-term effects of the decision? Did you pool your thoughts with your feeder programs to see if they were suffering from the same maladies? When the repair budget was cut for the orchestra, did you offer to share in the cuts? When your brothers in arms needed you, were you there for them? If not, then why would they be there for you?

Michael says,

> John Burn is more than my best friend; he is my brother. He is more than just the band director down the street (Homestead High School); he is my confidant and sounding board. We try to get together at least once a week. Sometimes we meet for coffee, sometimes he invites me to his family dinners, and sometimes it's a beer after

our Thursday night rehearsals. We try not to talk too much shop, but inevitably, it creeps back in. His students know me, and my students know him, and through it all he has helped me to be a better teacher and a better person.

The ever increasing demands of test scores and academic accountability have driven decision makers to make choices that stand in direct conflict with the very survival of our programs. This data obsession, combined with the economic climate, has created a perfect storm for those of us struggling to survive. As music teachers, we are battling both in classrooms and administration buildings for our professional lives. Instead of discussing them in a way that builds bridges, we look for our armory and ammunition, hoping to slow the advance of the enemy. But diplomacy and dialogue are far better solutions that leave both sides better for the wear, not to mention the students in our trust.

> We **must** reach out to our parents.
> We **must** reach out to our students.
> We **must** reach out to our community.
> We **must** reach out to our colleagues.
> We **must** connect with people.

Michael says convincingly,

> This is why we created a communal booster group. All instrumentalists from all grades in all schools speak with one voice and are centered

around one belief. Not only does it create a genuine sense of community, but allows for continuity from one program to another and one administration to another. Our job is to help people understand the importance of what we do rather than fight them over it.

Professional isolationism is an antiquated and unrealistic approach, yet as music teachers it is the approach we so often take. As our workload increases and we engage in the never-ending battle to meet professional and communal expectations, we dive deeper into our workload and become less accessible to those around us. We communicate and coordinate less and less often with those who seek to be of service and assistance. More than ever before, in our hyper-connected world music educators are caught standing alone in a crowded room of people willing to help. As we stand poising or poisoning ourselves for martyrdom, we spend more time planning for our memorial statue than we do meeting with our allies and working on solutions.

> My students aren't leaders.
> My parents aren't involved.
> My administrators don't understand what I do.
> My community doesn't support me.

Really?

As music educators we have the unique opportunity of being surrounded by people who, to a great extent, share our vision, beliefs, and goals. As educators we have the unique opportunity to be the sole vendors of musical information. At many schools the music department meeting could be held with a quorum of one because we are the only ones. Because of this, at many schools the decision-making process regarding music education occurs in a vacuum. Sure, many of us have boosters, but we relegate them to tasks and raising money. So we have these people around us who can be a resource that we so desperately need, and they are often scratching their heads, wanting to help but lacking the capacity or understanding to do so. We are unique in our standing because we are unique in our positions. When I asked Michael about this, he smiled and said,

> The first time I really understood this was my first year at Saratoga High School. The band was not particularly good, but was better than in recent years. I programmed Frank Ticheli's *Amazing Grace*, thinking it was an achievable goal. Through more of an accident of events, I discovered that there were three grandparents of students who were survivors of World War II. I asked them to come to the concert and speak of their experiences as a prelude to the performance. It was a transformative experience, not just for me and my students, but for our relationship with the community. This was my first experience with the contextual greatness of our art form. That moment changed the direction

and trajectory of our program, not because of the notes and rhythms we played, but because of the dialogue that it evoked among our school community.

On every campus, the English and Math departments are fortified by both strength and numbers, and can dictate the outcome of the school-wide decision-making process. Backed by the long arm of the law (curricula) and the strength of popular opinion, these two departments are the power brokers when it comes to issues relating to curricula and instruction. The numbers are clear for one and all to see, and the fight is anything but fair. While most schools have one, perhaps two music instructors, the faculty of the English and Math departments often number twenty-five or more. Given these odds, we become suspicious and reclusive rather than informed and engaged. We revel in our aloneness while we stand among the masses. But we have a support system that is the secret envy of every teacher and administrator on campus.

The English department doesn't have a booster group. The English department doesn't have representatives from local vendors visiting them weekly. The English department doesn't have a website, or a crowded auditorium of parents hanging on their every word. The Math department doesn't have students wearing tee shirts, ball caps, or patches on jackets proudly displaying their allegiance to polynomial equations. People don't attend math competitions in hopes of seeing artistry and achievement meet head on. The Math department doesn't have national organizations designed for advocacy. Yes, math teachers attend professional development conferences, but these offer teaching techniques, and not much in the way of community. Think about it: why do you attend your state conference or the Midwest Clinic? Is it because of the information or the connections? Are you equally passionate about the content as you are the context?

To my way of thinking, the English and Math departments stand alone and should be envious of us. Yes, in a faculty meeting their voices are daunting, but in a football stadium they are feeble. We have resources at our beck and call to address virtually any situation. We fail when we fail to use them! Our safety and salvation lies in our ability to establish relationships and connect to the people who are passionate about what we do and the young people we do it with. Michael Boitz saw that and acted on it from day one.

Michael says,

> As I mentioned earlier, one of the first things I did at Saratoga was reformat the way we dealt with our parent booster groups. My middle school feeder teacher, Vicki Wyant, was so inspirational with her love of her students and community, and I wanted to foster that at the high school. Eventually, we decided to join forces in pursuit of the same cause.

> Even though we are spread across two different districts, we have one booster organization. This group services every student in instrumental music from kindergarten through high school graduation. The board understands and advocates for the bigger picture of all music students regardless of age or where they go to school.
>
> When we started the concept it was a small band of merry brothers, but now the group has evolved into a force within our community and controls a budget that is well in excess of six figures. The board truly is one huge conglomerate of interconnected people with the same belief about music education. Our vision is to increase participation in music by young and old alike throughout our city.

When I asked Michael how they got started, he answered with the following:

> The best way to connect with those who do not understand what it is we do is through performance. We can talk to people until we are blue in the face, but when they see kids perform, it communicates far better than words. We make it a point to have our students, elementary and secondary alike, solos and ensembles, performing

as often as possible. When they perform, we have a list of requirements for the host to ensure that the performance setting has educational merit and that the kids are treated with respect and have a good experience.

Music teachers hang out; music teachers chat; music teachers gossip; music teachers vent… but music teachers don't connect. Many of us do not even connect with fellow music teachers in our very own school; instead, we find ourselves building walls against the very people that can help us the most. When information and alignment can make us stronger, we choose isolation. I am not sure if we fear other groups outperforming us or if we fear our peers seeing our weaknesses, but the end result is the same. We are comfortable displaying our performance product, but sheepish about sharing the process that created them. It appears that we would rather be wrong alone and right and in the company of the masses. But the problem is that being wrong alone does not lead to solutions, just repetition of the problem. The only way to fix something that is wrong is to let it see the light of day.

We are no different outside of the profession. We look to parents to sew, sell, and chaperone, but when it comes to advocacy and advancing the agenda of the program, instead of calling out the guard we cower in our offices and complain to our friends about the lack of support we have. The numbers are clear and in our favor. With high numbers of students, organized and informed parents, a national constituency of peers, and a retail industry in support of our success, the sheer thought of approaching a music program with the idea of cuts should give any administrator pause to think, and yet it doesn't. Everyone from NATO to the Teamsters has figured out that when the many stand as one, the one becomes stronger. Michael says,

> Aesthetic education is the most important and most lacking area of our public education. They are the most connected, hard working and enduring kids in school. However, I don't think that we as music teachers are great models of this.

Through his skills sets, Michael Boitz has created an interconnected web of involvement and understanding the likes of which few have seen. When the governing board made decisions that were contrary to the success of his program, the boardroom was filled with a sea of red band shirts demanding accountability. When the marching band unveiled their new uniform during a Monday night rehearsal, the town council showed up, including the mayor. When recent elections brought four new candidates to the ballot, they all asked for an official endorsement from "the Boitz." Michael's ability to connect with his students and his community has brought him political and professional clout that he uses as currency for the advancement of his program and students. He comments,

> In working with my community, I had to be able to see what's there and what's not. In the cultural context of the Asian community there is poverty.

It goes unnoticed because they have their basics met. It is a poverty of warmth and displays of love. Depending on how you look at it, Saratoga is just as much a fairy tale as it is an emotional ghetto, lacking in the basic communication of feelings among family members. This sense of isolationism, even in the home, is as much a part of our culture as anything else and I had to embrace and address it through music.

Never was this more apparent than in the case of Ruth Chiu. Many years ago, Lancy's sister, Ruth, was an active and engaged orchestra student. As the sister of someone so gregarious, it was hard to understand why Ruth was so quiet and unassuming. It was as if she actively worked at making no effort to stand out or call attention to herself. Like many siblings of his students, Michael knew Ruth from her frequent visits to the complex in search of her sister. They had spoken on many occasions but their relationship was no different than the hundreds of other non-music students that crossed his path every single day. Michael knew Lancy was active in speech and debate, but had no idea how gifted she was until one warm spring day.

Since Michael's program commands the largest multipurpose facility on campus, the sponsor from the school's highly successful speech and debate club asked if they could use the music facility for a mini assembly. Michael agreed and even offered to bring his class to watch the performances as a show of support. What he witnessed during that assembly still haunts him to this day. Lancy Chiu performed a solo monologue that was both artistic and revealing.

> I remember thinking that the pain she revealed through her character was more than just a performance and was altogether too real. It was almost disturbing to see that kind of emotion on display and struck me to the core. In the hours and days afterward, I struggled with the chasm between the Lancy that I knew—pleasant, quiet, and demure—with the person she revealed in her performance: struggling, depressed, and in a tremendous amount of pain.

> To better gauge the accuracy of my thoughts, I asked my students and even the club sponsor about theirs. To a person, they all saw it as an amazing performance, but gave no indication that it was anything more. I was mollified, but not convinced. Days later, during our city's annual Art Fair, on a beautiful spring afternoon, Lancy gathered her favorite things, sat on the lawn of our local college performing arts center, and swallowed enough pills to end her life.

> I will never forget the way our students responded in the aftermath of the tragedy. Beyond performing at Lancy's funeral, they

acted as a support group for her family and for each other. It was clear that these students needed connections and weren't getting them at home. Their outlet for emotions was music and each other. For me, the experience was a sort of looking glass, a true measure of what had been created in my few short years, as well as a clear picture of what was still left to be done.

During this time, unbeknownst to the students, Michael was preparing to leave Saratoga to pursue an advanced degree. He had already been accepted for his graduate work and had turned in his letter of resignation. That day, everything changed. He witnessed a transformative event. Right in front of his eyes, he saw his students step outside of their cultural heritage and try to connect with those in need. They didn't know what to do; they didn't know what to say. How could they? Even if they had, communication and sharing emotions ran contrary to everything they knew and had been taught. Their Eastern culture kept them confined within acceptable emotional parameters, and here they were, breaking through those historical and familial barriers in search of a way to help a friend in need. Michael says,

> In the aftermath of Lancy's death, seeing these students open up for the first time, seeing how far they had come and still yet, how far they had to go, I knew my work here wasn't done and was, in fact, just beginning. I walked to the front office and rescinded my letter of resignation.

Michael's eyes welled up with tears as he told the story, revealing and reliving the pain. It is almost as if Lancy's passing had just occurred. I got the sense that he felt some regret and responsibility. During that in-school performance, in that moment, in his room, in front of his eyes, he had connected with her. He saw through her performance facade and into her emptiness. He saw the true Lancy Chiu, devoid of happiness and alone in the world. He saw what others could not or would not see. He heard her cry as real and saw her tears as true. He knew all of this, and yet did nothing. I believe that with his gift comes a responsibility most of us will never know. In this case, ignorance is bliss, and knowledge comes with incredible responsibility.

As teachers we are in the people business. Our job is to facilitate experiences and the transfer of information. We are a musical eighteen-wheel semi, barreling down the highway, with a tractor-trailer full of information and ready to deliver. Our students are in need of our wares, but often close the access road that leads to them. So there we sit, at an impasse, motionless, with our impressive vehicle and cargo which has little-to-no value to those in need. It is then that we come to the realization that what we have to offer may be secondary to how we offer it. In other words, connections are sometimes more important than content. Maintaining open roads of communication with the people around you is more than just an analogy; it is a requisite for success. The journey of teaching and learning is dependent on the condition of the pathways between our students and ourselves, and we are in charge of maintaining these roads.

Those around Michael speak with unanimity about his success as a teacher and leader of young people. He is beloved beyond description and is seen as a permanent fixture, both on the faculty of Saratoga High School and in the general community. They can't imagine him anywhere but right where he is. Michael however, sees things a little differently.

> I have a secret desire to go teach music in an inner-city school. A place where no one else wants to teach and where students see music as more than just an activity but also as a coping mechanism for survival.

When I point out how different that world would be from the one of privilege and academia that he lives in now, he responds,

> There is more that connects us as people than separates us, and if you are willing to take the first step, connecting with people is easier than you might think. We *all* have something in common, and even if we don't, we can connect through music.

Chapter Five

SIX DEGREES FROM KEVIN BACON

On connecting with peers with Dr. Nola Jones of the University of Tennessee, Martin

"Hello?"

"May I please speak to Scott?"

The drawl of the woman's accent was so thick it was hard to tell exactly what she was saying at first. My first thought was that it was obviously a telemarketer, and a bad one at that. Either that or Scarlett O'Hara had just risen from the dead and was crank-calling me. So defined was her voice that I practically waited for her to start the next sentence with "Y'all, I do declare..." It was clear that whoever was on the other end of this phone call was not from anywhere I had ever lived. Although our conversation to this point had only consisted of six words, I knew instantly that this was someone I didn't know and was not likely to hear from again. As I am wont to do with telemarketers, I decided it was time to have some fun! I now had her in my auditory sights and was dreaming of the route to take as I pictured myself sitting on the veranda of a southern estate, complete with magnolia trees in full bloom and a servant delivering warm chocolate chip cookies and a ice cold glass of lemonade or sweet tea.

"This is he," I answered.

"My name is Nola Jones. I am interested in a position at Northern Arizona University. A mutual friend of ours, Terry Jolley, said I should give you a call and get some more information."

I was simultaneously intrigued and disappointed. Gone was the opportunity to amuse myself for a few brief moments, but I was curious to hear more about her and why she was calling me. Terry Jolley *was* a good friend of mine, and certainly anyone he would call a friend would be a friend of mine. I would later find out that our connection was irrelevant. After spending five minutes with her, everyone calls Nola a friend.

We hit it off instantly and spent nearly an hour on the phone that night. I was as charmed by her southern drawl as I was her charisma and knowledge. Through our banter, I was able to quickly surmise she had some serious game as an educator and was equally comfortable on the podium and the marching field. She had spent time as a high school teacher, college professor, drum corps judge, and more.

She asked all the right questions about the position, its history, and expectations. Her disarming drawl allowed her to ask pointed questions and yet made you feel like you were having a nice chat, when in fact you were sitting in a virtual hot seat. We discussed everything from the state of music education to the state of Tennessee. Our conversation was as effortless as it was enjoyable. By the end of the conversation I knew that she would not only be a good fit for the job she was seeking but also a good friend if and when she took the position. We exchanged pleasantries and contact info and I encouraged her to contact me if she had any other questions. I also told her to look me up when she got to town and I would hook her up with some "real" Mexican food if she was daring enough.

As the conversation came to a close, she stammered for the first time, almost hesitant to ask the final question.

"Can I ask you one last thing?" she asked.

"Sure, anything," I replied.

"I hear that they are interviewing just one other person. Some young hot-shot for the position," (her words, not mine).

"Do you know who it is... or can you tell me something about him?"

"I think I can," I said as I pondered the implications of my answer.

"I don't want to pry... just curious," she said, almost as an excuse to fill the noticeable void in the conversation.

"Well... I think the person you are talking about... is... me," I said. "I am certainly no hot-shot, and you could be describing someone else, but I have been contacted and asked to interview for the position."

She apologized instantly and assured me that she didn't know that when she called. It was merely the act of someone reaching out to a mutual acquaintance in search of information. She searched for the polite words to thank me for my time and yet end this conversation as quickly as possible to avoid any appearance of impropriety. I assured her that we were both victims of chance and that just as I had not known who she was when the phone rang, there was no way for her to know who I was, either.

As the nervous giggles that often accompany sticky conversations dissipated and we once again began the process of extracting ourselves from our conversation, she said,

"You mean that all this time you have been giving me information, you knew that you were in line for the same position?"

"Yes," I said.

"Well, aren't you just the sahweeetest thang?"

And there it was. With that one sentence, I had crossed the line. I had entered Nola's world, a place of professional connections so diverse and expansive that she is the sun in a virtual solar system of professional planets. You may not know Nola Jones, but I assure you, you know someone who does. Kevin Bacon has nothing on this woman, and I am convinced that given the opportunity she could simultaneously charm him out of his guitar, fix his bad tone, and convince him to get a haircut, all the while making him feel good about himself. This is Nola Jones' magic: the art of connecting with people on a very real and endearing level. She pulls no punches and isn't shy about what she thinks, but is so genuine in her concern for you and our profession that you cannot help but lower your defenses and allow her in.

"As kind as that was," she says,

> …there are tons of people in our profession who would have done the same thing as you did. You are not an anomaly. That is the beauty of what we do and who we are as a profession. There are so many people who are willing to help if people would just ask. Music education is filled with giving people who would do anything to help. The best teachers in the world are the ones who pick up the phone the most.

* * *

This petite dynamo was destined for music, and just looking at her, it is hard to conceive that she has been at it for over twenty-five years. She is youthful, energetic, and a marvel to watch. She has the passion of a new teacher and the experience of a veteran, and can make any group better in minutes. She packs the will and wallop of a linebacker into her four-foot eleven-inch frame with room to spare. It is even more difficult, knowing her, to conceive of what she must have been like as a young teacher, or even a small child. If age slows you down, then I am scared for the energy Nola Jones must have had as a first year teacher. As someone who is approaching her thirtieth year, Nola's passion and charisma are exhausting to watch; but even more impressive is how it all seems so effortless to her. I don't know where she finds her endless energy for teaching, but I do know that she was raised with love in her heart and music in her life. I know this because she still speaks to her parents every single day and she credits them with all she has become as a musician and teacher. You see, her mother was a concert pianist and her father was a drummer.

> They had a shared passion for music which took them and me wherever they went. They ended up in Chicago at Northwestern University where my father played in John Paynter's first band. Can you believe that? This was the first time he had to learn a real instrument and not just fool around on the drums. He was not allowed to major in percussion, so he chose the clarinet and pursued his music degree. Not only did he learn a new instrument, but he went on to study with members of the Chicago Symphony. My mother already had her degree in music so, to make ends

meet she proofread *The Instrumentalist*. After earning their degrees, my parents moved back to the South where they taught band together for over thirty years.

Regardless of where they were living at the time, Nola Jones was born and raised to be a southern woman. Full of warmth and charm, her genteel demeanor and unmistakable voice make you think you are talking to someone straight out of a Margaret Mitchell book. A tenacious spirit with people skills to match, she seemed destined to teach something if not music. After graduating from Mississippi State she started the band program at Heritage Academy in Columbus, Mississippi. Even as a first year teacher it was obvious that Nola understood the power of connecting with kids and its importance as a teaching tool.

> The room at Columbus was long and narrow, kind of like an airplane. They called it a "portable," but I called it a double-wide trailer. It was not a great classroom for band, as the only way to teach in it was to face the kids lengthwise. While this was contrary to everything I had been taught, I had no choice. I set the kids up in rows of two with an aisle down the middle. This allowed me to walk down the center of the room and easily get to each and every kid. Every day the group rotated their seats forward by one row so that every student would eventually be in the

front. This allowed me to not only hear them as individuals but see them as individuals.

Through this, I got to know each kid on a very personal level. Some of the kids that I started are now successful band directors. Sometimes I get chills when I see them walking the halls of the Midwest Clinic or when I see them at contest. This is when you know that you got it right. The exponential nature of teaching is one of the things I love about it. Seeing students you started become teachers of students, who will one day see their students become teachers themselves. Connecting with these people truly are some of my most treasured memories.

Nola defines herself by the people who surround her. She can connect with that ten-year-old child just as easily as she will twenty years later when they are teaching their own students. While time and circumstances change, she remains the same. She stands firmly rooted in her professional and personal values and is as open with her failures as she is her successes. She sees the person behind the performer and is unrelenting in her desire to see them succeed in whatever endeavor they pursue, both as a musician and a person. Once you are connected to Nola, you are connected to her for life; and a friend for life doesn't mean email exchanges, it means lots of hugs.

We live in a world of uber-connectivity that was almost unimaginable even five years ago, much less five decades ago. What was once the fodder for science fiction books in now the reality of our lives. Technology is growing at an exponential rate and is changing not only our lives but our classrooms. Our communication options have gone from the absurd to the incredulous. Where once there were few options other than a handwritten or typed letter and a phone call, now there exists a menu of possibilities that would make Ronald McDonald envious.

With the advent of the smartphone, communication once viewed as warp-speed now seems painfully slow. Our technological progress has placed text messaging and social networking at the forefront of our agenda and have made cell phone calls obsolete. Think about it: in the time it takes you to dial one person, you could have texted your entire database of friends or Twittered an entire worldwide network. Websites gave way to podcasts, which gave way to RSS feeds, which are now deemed as slow and antiquated. With the likes of Facebook, texting, and Twitter, email seems almost archaic. The thought of actually using pen, paper, and stamps is physically painful. In the time that it takes to write, proof, publish, and read this book, my once-hip and trendy references will date it and make it seem arcane. Our world and our words are now delivered via a multimedia, multi-platform method that allows the end user to analyze, sort, and act on information without ever leaving the confines of the home.

Regardless of your views or comfort level with technology, you can't deny that it provides people greater access and opportunity for communication and information management. As our world becomes more densely populated and our ability to connect with it increases, so does our desire to shrink it into something manageable or comfortable. We want to think of our planet and its people as enormous and filled with possibilities while still feeling secure and significant in our small place in it. We need to see elements such as war and human suffering as being far removed from us while seeing joy and happiness within our reach. We need in equal parts the possibility and grandeur of a huge planet while still feeling the proximity of intimacy of our own neighborhoods. We love large cities but live in small communities. We celebrate our country but are defined by our cities and neighborhoods. We need to feel that tragedy is distant and happiness is close. Nola says,

> Even in our profession, as enormous as it is, we want to feel connected. I belong to several educational groups that not only provide me with a professional outlet for growth but an environment of support and love from friends and colleagues. I know that not every music teacher has these opportunities and that it is more difficult in rural areas, but it still can be done and in today's day and age it is easier than ever before.

As a part of the human condition, we need to feel a sense of belonging. Maslow's hierarchy shows us the importance of this primal sense by placing love and belonging just after saftey and basic needs. Regardless of whether the belonging is personal or professional, our need for an identity is so deeply entrenched that it directs just about everything we do.

Take your job, for example. You are not a professional educator; that description would be far too vague and ambiguous. You are Director of Bands at (insert school name here). You have further defined yourself with a district, school, department, and program. Your voicemail greeting probably identifies not just you, but your program as well, as if dialing your number and reaching that voicemail wasn't a pretty good indicator that they already knew who you were.

I have also been amazed that many people's email signatures contain more characters than the Gettysburg Address. We wear logo-emblazoned polo shirts and have a set of business cards on the ready should anyone ask. These may appear to be the symbols of identification. In fact, they are symbols of association. According to Maslow, our desire to achieve success is subordinate to the desire to connect with the people involved in it. We want to be connected to our colleagues, our peers, and yes, our students. Believe it or not, we even desire to connect with those we perceive as "un-connectable"—hence the obsession many people have with celebrities and reality television.

Fueled in part by this desire and in part by sleep deprivation, three students at Albright College—Craig Fass, Brian Turtle, and Mike Ginelli—created the game *Six Degrees from Kevin Bacon*. According to an interview with their college newspaper in 1999, the trio were watching *Footloose* (a Kevin Bacon film) which was followed by another film starring Bacon: *Quicksilver*. Afterwards they began to speculate about how many movies Bacon had been in and the number of people he had worked with. The more they thought, they more they were amazed at the connections they were able to make.

In the interview, Brian Turtle said, "It became one of our stupid party tricks, I guess. People would throw names at us and we'd connect them to Kevin Bacon."

The trio wrote to talk-show host Jon Stewart stating that, "Kevin Bacon was the center of the entertainment universe," and explained the premise of the game. Needless to say, the game took off. Bacon admitted that he initially disliked the concept because he believed it was ridiculing him, but he eventually came to enjoy it. The three friends released a book, *Six Degrees of Kevin Bacon*, with an introduction written by the actor himself. Soon after, a board game based on the concept was released and has become a pop culture phenomenon.

In an effort to either quantify or debunk the six degrees of separation theory, researchers at Microsoft recently studied thirty billion text messages from one hundred and eighty million people in various countries. According to the *Washington Post*, this was the first time a planetary-scale study of social networking had been done. The researchers used the Microsoft Messenger network in June of 2006, which at that time was responsible for approximately half of the world's instant messaging traffic. Researchers Eric Horvitz and Jure Lescovec looked at the minimum number of chain lengths or steps it would take to connect one hundred and eighty billion different pairs of users. They concluded that seventy-eight percent of all users could be connected in less than seven steps (6.6 steps to be precise), thus validating the urban legend of six degrees of separation. It turned out that these college friends stuck in a snow storm were closer to the truth than they had originally thought. What started as a party game in fact became a universal truth. Virtually speaking, you and I are connected to each other whether you like me or not. You are almost kinfolk to Brad Pitt and Angelina Jolie, and I am seriously considering asking Jon Bon Jovi to feed my goldfish while I am on vacation next month. Man... am I popular or what? Nola says,

> Being connected to your peers is so critical to your success, especially as a young teacher. I don't care who you are and where you live, there are opportunities to connect and spend time with people who can help you get better. Sure, it's easier for some because of proximity and geography, but it can still be done.

And Nola would know. She has taught public school in some fairly out-of-the-way places. In fact, for the bulk of her career, she has helped to create success in places that most of us would call remote. During her time in Arizona she was a three- to five-hour drive from most high schools, and yet she was one of the most visible and active clinicians in the state.

As music teachers, the advent of technology has allowed us to stay in better contact with the students we teach and their families. At an almost corollary rate, the distance between ourselves and other teachers seems to be growing larger. Communication comes at us so fast and in such volumes that, after a while, it becomes virtual white noise.

Our students are no different. They may stop listening to what we say because they know they can get the same information when they need it elsewhere. They stop interacting with their peers because they know that they can reach them later if need be. Having the ability to connect with your peers sometimes negates the desire to actually do so. That is one of the many wonders of music: it forces kids to interact socially and musically for long periods of time each and every day. Oh, if only it were true among music teachers.

With each new technological advancement we create a level of convenience that further trivializes and diminishes our need for real interaction, both professionally and personally. As digital voicemail, email, cell phones, video conferencing, and social networking have improved the convenience of communication, we use it less and less. As reaching our sister-school colleagues becomes easier, so does ignoring them.

It seems counterintuitive, but as the ease of communication increases, the quality and quantity of it decreases. I will be the first to admit that I have no empirical data to support this theory, but I have seen it too many times to believe it is just coincidence. Think back to a time before text messaging and emailing (if you can); to a time when you needed to borrow some literature from a colleague and had to go to their school to get it. That trip, as inconvenient as it was, would often result in the two of you talking about the strengths and weaknesses of the piece, sharing recordings and rehearsal techniques, and would allow you to see another organization outside of your own professional cocoon. Since it took effort to make the trip, you were more invested in the experience once you got there. You wanted to make sure that you had every part, multiple recordings, and asked every question in case you didn't get another chance.

It is as if we need separation to create attraction. Now, we typically scan, fax, or send the same material as an attachment to an email. Is this way more efficient? Absolutely! Is it more effective? I'm not convinced. It is the fifteen-second exchange of information with a colleague that becomes fifteen minutes that helps you to grow, not the fifteen-minute exchange that becomes fifteen seconds made more efficient through email. Just as teaching and learning begin and end with the person on the podium and the child in the seat, professional growth begins and ends not with the information but the people sharing it. Technology has made managing our programs infinitely easier, but has unintentionally had the opposite effect on us as people and teachers.

No curricula in education is as well connected as music. When it comes to students, we see them multiple hours a day, six days a week, for both semesters and over multiple years. Music educators have more opportunities to connect with students on a meaningful level than most other teachers in a school system. When it comes to professional encounters, we are far more aggressive than our educational counterparts. We see our colleagues and their collective body of work virtually every Friday night and/or Saturday afternoon. We attend professional development conferences, perform for each other at contest on a regular basis, have access to trade journals, clinics, web sites, recordings, and so much more. And with it all, as music teachers we tend to confuse what is most convenient with what is most beneficial.

As teachers, we may not want to be taught. In a people-centered profession, we tend to choose isolation. For this reason, as young teachers our professional development tends to come via trial by fire and not the exchange of information. What concerns me is not that we are more disconnected than our fellow teachers; it is that we have greater opportunities to remedy this and fail to capitalize on them.

> If we don't start connecting better, we are doomed. As someone who works with young teachers and teacher preparation, it is my job to see that we get that message across. There are so many reasons to reach out: inspiration, information, or just to have your batteries

> recharged. My philosophy is that music makes us more human, more loving, and makes our life experience more fulfilling. I can hear a recording of the Chicago Symphony Orchestra and it's wonderful, but it is not the same thing as seeing it. We need to share this connection through music to bridge the divide our world faces. If there was ever a time more than now when the world needed to be connected in more loving and tolerant ways, I was not alive to see it.

Nola is one of the few people who can not only see the chasms within our profession, but bridge them. She is equally at home on the concert podium as she is in the judges' box. She is almost as well known among the cast of characters in the drum corps world as she is at Bands of America. During her career she has successfully taught at every educational level (elementary, middle school, high school, and college) and in a variety of economic and demographic settings.

> Wherever I went, people did it for me. They led me around and introduced me. You just have to find yourself a mentor and attach yourself to them at the hip when you attend functions. The rest will take care of itself. You don't have to be the life of the party, but you do have to be willing to go to the party. Having people near you who can help you grow but ignoring them is like having oil on your land but doing

> nothing with it. It doesn't do anything to enhance your life.
>
> I'm sure that some of it is my personality, but the rest is just a choice. Anyone can do it. You just have to work at it. Is it hard? Sure it is, but you have to do it. There are people I am scared to approach. I get star-struck too, but I do it anyway. I mean, how can you not? For me, I will never forget when I met Maya Angelou, Frederick Fennell, Ray Cramer, and John Paynter.

Nola learned her bold ways at a very young age from her father.

> I was virtually a first-year teacher and my groups were working on *Prelude, Siciliano and Rondo* by John Paynter. I was having trouble understanding the piece, so I called my father for some advice. He blew me off as if to say, "Why are you calling me?" He told me to call John Paynter and ask him myself. I was just young and dumb enough to pick up the phone and do it. John spent over an hour on the phone with me explaining the piece and giving me some hints. I learned a big lesson that day and vowed to never again shy away from asking for help.

> Music educators don't share enough. I am not sure why, but it might be because we are scared. Some say that it's because of competition, but I just don't agree. I think it's fear. I think we are afraid to admit that we don't know something. I think we are afraid to admit to a lack of knowledge or that we have weaknesses. It just doesn't make sense to me. I mean, if you felt bad and had a temperature of 104 degrees, would you go to the doctor? Of course you would. But when it comes to needing expert advice in our own profession, we ignore the people who have the answers.

To make her point, she tells a story.

> I went to a clinic not that long ago on rehearsal techniques for woodwinds, and standing in front of the room was a master teacher who had successfully taught band at the collegiate level for over thirty years. He is a living legend both as a conductor and pedagogue. He could play every single woodwind instrument with equal proficiency. I mean, he is truly a master teacher. And there we were in this clinic, just him, me, and one other person who wasn't even a teacher. It is a shame to think of all of the knowledge he had and was willing to share and only an empty room to hear it.

You asked me if I think that we collaborate enough. I don't think it is possible to collaborate enough. I don't think you can ever ask enough questions or attend enough clinics, and I think the really good directors know that. I don't think we can ever meet enough people, attend enough rehearsals, or watch enough groups, and I think that the people we would call successful are successful because they know what they don't know and are willing to get some help. All I know is that there are people out there who can help me, and I am going to talk to them.

Sometimes I don't understand our profession. If we aren't observing, helping, and talking to one another, we are making our jobs harder. Why would you do that? Why would you compromise yourself and your students' experience that way? Would we teach by standing on one leg with our hands tied behind our back? No, of course we wouldn't. It would make things more difficult and wouldn't yield any benefit. The same thing is true here. We are so busy worrying about the next concert, or preparing the next application for a special event that we lose sight of what and whom we are doing it for.

Think about the past week. How many colleagues have you spoken with? I am not talking about idle chit-chat or the brief conversation while picking up your mail. I am talking about a conversation you initiated with the sole intent of trying to be better at something. If the answer is less than what you would like, then ask yourself why? What do you have to lose? Not only can conversations like this reinvigorate your teaching, but they can awaken your spirit and stoke the passions that drove you to be a teacher in the first place. These conversations remind us of what we aspire to be and are every bit as important for us as they are for our students. Nola says,

> Our profession is not one filled with the riches of money, but we are rich beyond belief with our time and our talent, and that is the most precious gift you can give to someone else or yourself.

The gift of time is one you have to be willing to give as well as receive. As music educators we are in a state of crisis. For years music education has seen an alarming decrease in the number of qualified applicants for positions. This does not imply that the applicant pool is not of quality, but that the pool of potential candidates is dwindling. Making matters worse, music teachers are leaving the profession in staggering numbers that can't be explained simply by retirement. Teachers are leaving the profession because they are unhappy, and those who are most at risk are those to whom the future belongs: young teachers.

Statistically speaking, our youngest teachers are at the greatest risk for failure and are most likely to leave before having a true understanding of how to succeed in this complex profession. According to recent studies, seventeen percent of first-year music teachers will not return for year two. Thirty-two percent will not teach beyond their third year and a full half of all young teachers will not see the inside of a classroom after five years. The national teacher-to-student ratio for music is two hundred and eighty students to every one teacher, and those who are getting instruction may not be receiving from a highly qualified source. According to the Music Educator's National Conference, twenty-seven-million school children are being taught by unqualified or under-qualified teachers. Solving this problem is paramount to our professional survival and the well-rounded education of America's children.

With each and every passing day, the task of being a music teacher becomes more difficult, more voluminous, and more isolating. The learning curve once associated with success has now become a right angle. Run as hard as you can, crash into a wall, and either go upward and continue on your path, injured and confused, or turn around and quit in anger and frustration. Unless young teachers experience some success in their early years, they will not return, leaving the students of the music program to start all over again with another new teacher. It is like a bad composition with a repeat sign at the end. We just keep playing it over and over.

* * *

In a study commissioned by the National Association for Secondary School Principals, it was discovered that having a qualified mentor with dedicated time to spend was the most important factor in young teacher development and retention. If we are to stem the tide of retreat and turn around these dismal numbers, we have to find a way to connect new teachers with established mentors. As the ranks of music educators grow closer to retirement and remaining teachers dwindle, the shallowness of the applicant pool will lead to a lack of effective and evolving educators and compromise the quality of our music education system. More than ever before, students need experienced, effective, and engaged teachers. I firmly believe that the greatest threat to music education is our lack of effort to foster relationships within our profession. These relationships can help guide the young and inexperienced in our pack through the survival process and into leadership positions where they can do the same for others. As professional music teachers, we fight for the right of every student to have a qualified music educator as a part of their school experience, but do very little if anything to ensure that we have someone to fill that role. We need to do a better job of connecting with our younger colleagues, if not for them, for ourselves and our students.

The time is now, and the clarion call of survival has been sounded for one and all to hear. It is time to connect with our professional heroes. It is time to reach out and stretch ourselves. It is time to put down the computer keyboard and visit a colleague. It is time to use technology not to entertain us but to enrich us. It is time to connect with those who know less as well as those who know more. It is time to schedule a clinician or guest conductor, or be one!

Visit another rehearsal. Set up an exchange concert. Sign up to attend a clinic. Post something on a music education message board. Send a request for professional development to your district office. It is time to stand united, not just as a profession but as a community which shares our passion for music and what it teaches our children. It is time to expand our horizons to the district, regional, state, and national level.

"It will be difficult, but it can be done and *must be done*," said Nola.

Having heard that, it seemed as if our time together and interview was coming to a close. It had been hours and yet felt like minutes. It was a joy to spend time with someone who I enjoy and admire simultaneously. In response to a gut feeling, I asked Nola if I could see her cell phone.

"Why? You have a phone right there and it's nicer than mine. Besides, I don't get very good reception in here," she said in a dismissive tone.

"Never mind that. Can I see it?" I said.

I explained that I wasn't looking to make a call, but I wanted to see her address book. She looked at me quizzically and reluctantly handed it over. As I fumbled through an unfamiliar interface and worked my way through her electronic phone book, I found a veritable *Who's Who* list of our profession: composers, conductors, teachers, and corporate music giants alike were listed side by side as if they all played for the same team—Nola's team. When I asked her who was on her speed dial, she told me that she didn't know how to program it, but if she did, she said it would be her momma and daddy, as she connected with them every single day.

I asked her how many names were in her address book.

> I don't know, but I had to delete a bunch because I got a new phone and it said the memory card was full and couldn't hold any more names. I struggled with this more than you know. My phone was telling me to delete people. How could I do that? Its not like they are just names; they are people, they are my friends.

Her memory is not the only thing that is full; so is her heart. And with that comment, I posed my last question: "If you needed to, could you find Kevin Bacon in six steps or less?"

She began to gather her things. She smiled as if to imply that she appreciated the irony of the question but wasn't going to answer it.

So I asked it again.

As Nola placed her napkin on the table signifying the end to our lunch and interview, she leaned in towards me and lowered her voice as if she was revealing something truly embarrassing and said,

"I'm not sure, but... I have a cousin who was an art director on his last movie, so I guess, I could make a phone call and... well..."

And there it was, plain for the world to see. We are all just six steps away from each other. So I left, feeling a lot better about music education, and a little bit better about the world and my place in it, as I was now just *three* degrees away from Kevin Bacon, which I guess you could say means that you are now *four*.

Congratulations!

Chapter Six

Leonardo da Vinci and the Chocolate Chip Cookie
On being a professional with Scott Rush of Wando High School

For over five hundred years the works and writings of Leonardo da Vinci have captivated scholars, artists, and historians alike. More than just a man, he was a scientist, mathematician, engineer, inventor, anatomist, painter, sculptor, architect, botanist, musician, and writer. Da Vinci has often been described as the archetype of the Renaissance man, one whose unquenchable curiosity was equaled only by his work and inventions. He is widely considered to be one of the greatest painters of all time and perhaps the most diversely talented person ever to have lived.

Beyond that, Leonardo da Vinci was a person of mystery. His works are filled with ciphers, cryptic messages, and hidden meanings. The most well known of his works, the *Mona Lisa* and the *Last Supper*, have inspired private sleuths and amateur historians seeking the truths believed to be contained within these paintings. Yes, Leonardo da Vinci is among history's most brilliant thinkers and best secret keepers.

Scott Rush has a secret, too. A secret so dark and deep that perhaps even he doesn't know it. Anyone who has ever spent any time with him can see it, but for Scott, he wears his secret like the Emperor wears his new clothes. His secret is naked to the world but fully clothed in his own mind. Scott's secret is that he is smarter than the rest of us. Scott would blush at the hint of being in any way superior to anyone, but superior he is. Scott is wicked smart. Scott is "game show, win a million bucks, don't buy a car, put it in a high yield Roth 401K"-type smart. He is someone whose talents span the traditional boundaries of right brain/left brain that would leave most people confounded, and yes, he can keep a pretty good secret.

Beyond being a man of superior intellect, Scott is also hard working and places a premium on civility and honesty. He is a living, breathing, walking embodiment of the person my mother wanted me to be. Think about all of the times you screwed up; all of the times your parents threw their hands in the air and proclaimed to the high heavens that they just didn't know what to do with you and wished you would behave more like... (If you don't have any of these memories, feel free to call me, as I have a boatload of them, and I would be happy to channel my mother for you). If your parents had met Scott, I am sure he would be the comparison you loathed.

As an adult and a music teacher, he still fulfills this same arduous role. Every time I see him work or read a chapter in one of his books, I am reminded of the person and teacher

I should have and could have been. Not having followed Scott around for an entire day, I am left to imagine how he approaches his myriad of tasks and lists of things to do. Somehow I see him achieving all of the daily tasks that I wrestle with and fail to achieve.

- Early to bed, early to rise. (check)
- Make bed before leaving, hospital corners (check)
- Treat others how you wish to be treated (check)
- Work smarter, not harder (check)
- Learn something new (check)
- Wave hello to the person in traffic who just flipped you off (check)
- Rescue a small animal and return it to its natural ecosystem (check)
- Leave the world a better place than you found it (check)
- Help with household chores (check)
- Spend quality time with son (check)
- Check to-do list for uncompleted tasks (check)
- Floss (check)
- Sleep (check)
- Repeat (check)

And I imagine this idyllic lifestyle doesn't end at the band room doors.

- Check teacher mailbox twice a day (check)
- Say hello to all of the secretaries along the way (check)
- Smile at the custodians and thank them daily (check)
- Take attendance and keep good records (check)
- Lesson plan (check)
- Organize office (check)
- Music library alphabetized and inventoried (check)
- Respond to all emails and phone calls (check and double check)
- Un-jam the copier that someone else left (check)
- Rotate batteries in the tuners (check)
- Rotate baton usage (check)
- Re-carpet top of conductor's podium (check)

Apparently while I was fulfilling my responsibility to be as self-absorbed and self-loathing as possible, Scott was doing something else; he was being productive.

I know I am probably being a little Pollyanna or naive about all of this, but in my mind, this is how I see him. Scott is the teacher our college professors hoped we would be. Scott is the person your music education textbooks were talking about. In fact, Scott is the person that wrote the textbook! As I write this, I think I am getting a little angry. He is too good to be true, and in his "perfectness" he is making the rest of us look bad. In fact, I think we should all get together and lock him in an instrument locker and... well, maybe not. He would probably convince us that the "pen is mightier than the sword," and by the time he was done talking us to our senses, he would have us holding hands, sitting in a circle, and sightsinging melodic minor scales.

As a teacher, Scott is every bit the embodiment of the person one expects to see in a successful program. He is affable, kind, caring, sincere, and engaged. If you ask anyone around him, they will describe him as the consummate professional who is both demanding and loving toward his students. Scott has mastered both the mechanics and the artistry of teaching, and if that isn't enough, finds enough time to write two bestselling books about it and is working on a third.

Emily Jones, a music educator and former student of Scott's, describes him this way:

> When Mr. Rush is teaching, each word is important. Every conducting gesture is full of life, soul, and spirit. Mr. Rush's blood drips with music. I will never forget the four *Ts*: In Tune, in Time, Tone, and Technique. I try each day to teach my own band students with as much passion and music running through my veins as Scott Rush exuded when he taught me.
>
> He once told me never to forget that we are in the people business. Teaching lifelong lessons

through music is what being a band director is all about. He has earned the affection of his students because he cares for them like a father cares for his children.

Like Emily, many music educators have had someone in their lives that has had a similar effect on them. Someone caring and nurturing that took the extra time to guide them through the minefield that is the teenage years. In that respect, Scott Rush is not alone. In fact, in all probability, as you read this book, there is someone, somewhere who sees you in a similar light. She may not have told you as much, but she has thought it. You might even be surprised to know who it is. It may not be your best player. She may not even be particularly good, but nonetheless, she sees you in a special light. You have had a profound impact on her life.

I imagine that you have someone who has helped to shape you as well. Think about it. Close your eyes and picture his face. Try to hear the sound of his voice. What was it about him that made such an impact? Was it what he said or what he did? Was it what he taught or how he taught it? Many of us have a Scott Rush in our lives, someone who meant the world to us not just as a teacher but as a role model. As I said, in this area Scott stands in good company. What separates him from many of his peers is not what he does but the way he does it and how he prepares for it.

Scott Rush never intended to be a teacher. Despite growing up in a musical household, he was able to elude what to others seemed to be an obvious and natural career path. His choice seemed preordained, given the environment in which he was raised. Both of his parents were educators and even ended their careers teaching side by side. Even with such successful role modeling, he never aspired to follow in his parents' footsteps. He has a passion for music and the soul of an artist, but was never comfortable being the focus of attention. While this may seem contradictory for a performer to shy away from the spotlight, this is but one of the many contrasts to the qualities of a conventional teacher that Scott embodies. He is passionate about music and wants to be the source of the light and not the recipient of it. He wants to shine the light on his students.

As a teenager, his obsession with music was not confined to the band room. Scott worked the afternoon shift as a disc jockey.

> I had a friend, Jimmy Smith, who worked at radio station WCAM in our hometown. He was really good and went on to make it big-time in the radio world. The station manager asked Jimmy if he had any friends who might want to work part-time at the station. Jimmy recommended me and trained me, and I loved it. I started on the weekends and worked Saturday and Sunday afternoons from one to six PM. Then they put me on the afternoon drive time during the week when I could do it. It was a small enough situation that if I had a band function, someone else at the station would cover it.

I learned so much working at the station. There was so much freedom in creating the show. First of all, we could pick our own music (within a rotation system) and I definitely liked certain groups (especially Earth, Wind, and Fire). I also had lots of friends that listened, and it made for good conversation at school. I enjoyed working the sound/mixer board, because DJs used to have to cue up the records (45s) and segue all of the transitions into and out of commercials (on carts, which looked like old eight-track tapes). There was a lot that you had to do simultaneously and it was exciting. It's all done by computers now. Another thing that I liked was that most people who called in with requests knew nothing about me. I got all types of requests, including propositions from women who probably would have flipped if they had known I was in high school. I did use my real name, though.

Just as he was more comfortable in the small confines of a DJ booth than the open space of a classroom, Scott was far more content in a practice room than in front of an ensemble. He prefers the anonymity of it, and relishes creating music in both roles.

Even though he spun the vinyl, Scott was good enough to play on it. As a classically trained musician, Scott has received degrees in music performance from the University of South Carolina and the prestigious New England

Conservatory of Music, and no one who had ever heard him play would doubt his abilities. As a horn player few were his equal, and he achieved his success by practicing and playing with a systemic approach and dogmatic energy. He was successful by any account and his professional friends were more than a little surprised when he choose to start over again and become a teacher.

> In 1989 Mike Walters was head of the Music Education Department at the New England Conservatory when I was there. He was offered the Dean's job at Kennesaw State and he asked me if I would like to come there and teach horn as part of the adjunct faculty. In the same week, my college teacher, Bob Pruzin, phoned and said that there was a full-time woodwind quintet based in Atlanta called the Pandean Players and they were looking for a horn player. They wanted to know if I would go on tour with them and the tour was the audition for the job. After we completed the tour they offered me the position and I moved to Atlanta. I played with the Atlanta Ballet, the Augusta Opera, the Augusta Symphony, the Atlanta Symphony in the summer at Chastain Park, the Pandean Players, the Macon Symphony, and even drove to Columbia and Greenville, South Carolina when I could. In addition to teaching lessons to the horn majors that I had at Kennesaw, I taught private

lessons to some of the Cobb County kids at Pope and Lassiter High Schools and loved it. I hustled, but made a pretty decent salary. As a matter of fact, I took a pay cut to become a band director.

Initially, I loved the lifestyle of gigging for a living, but over time, it became more of a chore than a joy. I was also having trouble with some health issues associated with the stress of always being "on" and feeling that I had to be the perfect horn player. There's nowhere to hide in a professional woodwind quintet, and I put a great deal of pressure on myself to be good. The stress took it out of me and my playing became a job, not a passion. That was when I tried to evaluate whether I was truly happy and asked myself, "Is this what I'm going to be doing the rest of my life?" I then asked myself, "What makes you happiest right now?" And the answer was "Teaching the kids in Cobb County." In addition to teaching the private lessons, I taught a camp, and Gary Gribble at Pope High School asked if I would come out during the day and help. I went when I could and loved teaching the kids.

I enjoyed teaching the lessons and horn class at Kennesaw, but since I was an adjunct professor, I was very part-time. Even though I enjoyed this, there was always something in my gut that said that I'd love to teach young people and be a band director. I taught camps in the summer, I was a counselor at Brevard Music Center, and I also helped my old high school director with his camp. I was happiest teaching high school students.

To help him fulfill his new passion for teaching, he simultaneously taught and took classes at Kennessaw State while serving on the faculty and obtained his teaching credentials. Nearing his thirtieth birthday—an age when most people are looking for career advancement, not a new beginning—Scott walked away from everything he had worked for and known in the performance world to embark on a new career.

When most of us chose this profession we saw ourselves as artisans spending our days and nights crafting soaring melodies and dreaming up field productions of grandeur. Having no experience other than our own, most of us believed the skills sets required for success as a band director were as innate as they were esoteric. We thought that our success or failure would be more dependent on our conducting technique rather than our typing technique. We thought that our chosen profession of music education would give our creative spirit room to roam freely without the constraints of curricula associated with other subject areas. As music teachers, we believed our job was to see something where there was nothing, hear something where there was only silence, and build something where there was no blueprint. We believed that in the absence of everything, our success would hinge on our ability to create. We were auditory and visual sculptors, with young people and the printed score as our tools of creation. Then we started the job only to find out that we forgot to order the paint, the canvases are all dirty, and the sculptor's wheel has been broken for the past three years.

After stepping into our new role we quickly came to find that our real job was more akin to that of a custodian, bus driver, instrument repair person, webmaster, and hall monitor than that of orchestra conductor. We had to learn to be an effective and efficient program manager, inventory control specialist, transportation coordinator, and accountant, all the while trying to remember the copy code and which key opens what door. The job that we trained for required us to be able to read a score, but the job we found ourselves doing required us to read an excel spreadsheet. We were trained to be right-brained people who were working in a left-brained world. While it is unlikely that you are equally adept at using both parts of the brain with equal ease and dexterity, it is even more unlikely that you will be a highly successful teacher without being able to do so.

* * *

Scott Rush is one of the very few people I have ever met that can bridge the chasm between the worlds of instructional design (why and what we teach) and program management (when, where, who we teach). He navigates these two separate but equal worlds with relative ease and seems equally at home in both. He can discuss solo and ensemble repertoire in one breath and departmental budget issues in the next, and perhaps more importantly, he understands their symbiotic nature with alarming clarity and depth. Scott says,

> You put all the tools in the musical box, handle all of the professional responsibilities, you do everything well, but ultimately, to make the experience whole you have to get to the musical moment. Everything we do leads to that space in time.

I guess his secret of being smarter than us is not such a big secret after all. In fact, it's not even that unique, and might be misunderstood. I believe that his success is more a result of his balance than his genius. I know that Scott is an incredibly bright man, but I believe that his success is tied to the fact that he chooses to use both his analytical and artistic skills in pursuit of that very goal: success. We all know that there are two sides to our job, instructional and non-instructional. But we favor what we enjoy doing and ignore what we don't. Rather than face our nemesis, we say things like, "I'm not good at it," or, "It's not as important as kids." My personal favorite, though, is, "I just don't have enough time to get to that."

Scott always seems to have whatever time it takes to get the job done, and he does so with a genuine humility for what he does not know and a similar disdain for what he does not like to do. Scott does not shy away from what he does not enjoy; he just discards the excuses and gets it done so he can move on to other things. It's almost as if his logical brain can overrule his creative brain at will.

Most people are aware that the brain is divided into two separate, symmetrical, but different parts: the left and right hemispheres. Popular culture advocates the belief that we favor one side over another, but the truth is we are a combination of the two and could not live without either one or the one quadrillion neurons that connect them. Working seamlessly together, the hemispheres of the brain determine how we breathe, walk, talk, eat, process information, manage pain, sort through emotions, and so much more. Both sides are equally critical for maintaining even the most basic functions and thought patterns. However, there is a distinct difference in each side's sphere of control and responsibility over what we do and how we behave.

While this has been suspected to be the case since the early part of the twentieth century, only recently has it been proven and made quantifiable by the development of the Functioning Magnetic Resonance Image, which shows in real time where blood flows and the amount of electrical activity in the brain. Author Daniel Pink of the landmark book *A Whole New Mind: Why Right-Brainers Will Rule the Future* describes the differences between the operations of these separate but equal hemispheres in the following four ways:

1. The left hemisphere controls the right side of your body; the right hemisphere controls the left side of your body.
2. The left hemisphere is sequential; the right hemisphere is simultaneous.
3. The left hemisphere specializes in text; the right hemisphere specializes in context.
4. The left hemisphere analyzes the details; the right hemisphere synthesizes the big picture.

The world has long celebrated those who could not only make sense of little things, but how they connect to the bigger world in general. We are currently living in a right-brained world that that looks to and celebrates the logical and concrete. People who understand concrete and finite things—analysts, economists, and computer programmers—are in the greatest demand and are remunerated at the highest levels. However, without an understanding of the context of this information the meaningfulness of the content is compromised. In this way Scott Rush is unique. Not only is he comfortable discussing pedagogy, scope, or sequence on virtually any instrument, but can use these to create a great ensemble sound.

I venture to guess that, like Scott, many brilliant thinkers have an undervalued opinion of their prowess.

Driven in part by humility and in part by an understanding of what they *don't* know, it is often difficult when dealing with people of this intellect level to distinguish between self-doubt and self-deprecation. Scott Rush also has an undervalued sense of self worth, in part because he does not understand that it is not what he thinks but how he thinks that makes him so extraordinary.

In Michael J. Gelb's book, *How to Think Like Leonardo da Vinci*, we learn more about da Vinci and his notable approach to thinking called The Seven Sciences. By understanding his approach to learning we can better understand someone whose genius spans many levels and is involved in whole-brain thinking. This is what made da Vinci so exceptional and this is what makes Scott Rush such an effective teacher. Like Leonardo da Vinci, Scott Rush takes a whole-brain approach to music education.

Noted scholars have come to the belief that da Vinci's extensive writings reveal seven distinct principals required for developing your whole brain and inner genius.

Curiosità	Be curious about everything around you.
Dimostrazione	Demonstrate through your own experience. Think for yourself.
Sensazione	Sharpen your senses, the secret to enjoying life and savoring it.
Sfumato	Be open to the unknown and willing to embrace uncertainty.

Arte/Scienza	Balance art and science, logic and imagination. Leonardo said, "Study the science of art and the art of science."
Corporalità	Balance your mind and body. In addition to being an artistic and scientific genius, Leonardo was physically gifted. He emphasized the importance of diet and positive attitude and the effect of that positive attitude on health and well-being.
Connessione	Realize that everything connects to everything else. Look for ways to transfer your knowledge from one area to another.

As I look at Scott Rush and the skills sets he uses to build success at Wando High School, I see a man who is a whole-brain thinker. He is someone who can balance the demands of both art and analytics. He is someone who doesn't see non-teaching demands as distractions but as an important part of the overall puzzle. Scott enjoys both the process of making music and building the support structure around it.

If we examine da Vinci's seven sciences and apply them to Scott Rush's teaching style, we are better able to identify and observe how and why he has been able to achieve such success.

Curiosità: Be curious about everything around you.

Scott is a student of music education. He constantly strives to better understand not only the art of it, but the science of it. He is thoughtful and insightful and can absorb information at an alarming rate. He is a voracious reader and consumes multiple books at one time.

When I asked him what was on his nightstand right now, he told me he was reading Frank Battisti's *On Becoming A Conductor* and was re-reading *On Becoming a Better Leader* by Warren Bennis. When I asked him why he was re-reading the Bennis book he responded:

> When I read it the first time, I was young and inexperienced. I think I missed a lot because I didn't have the framework of understanding to grasp it. I haven't read a book for pleasure in twenty years. If I am reading something, it is to make me a better teacher or a better person.
>
> In order to understand that statement, you have to understand how bad I was at teaching when I started. About eight days into my first teaching job I called in sick and spent the entire day reading the help wanted section of the paper. I thought I was terrible at teaching, and I was right. If you asked me about my worst day, I would tell you to pick any given day during that first year. I didn't know what I was doing. There were times when I said some ugly things or used

some choice words. On one day in particular, after one of my tirades, my first chair flautist, a thirteen-year-old girl who went to my church looked up at me and said, "Pitiful... just pitiful."

That is a moment I will never forget, although she would. Years later, after serving as my drum major, she went on to college and got married. At her wedding, I asked her if she remembered that day and thanked her for the profound effect she had on me. She said that she did not remember that day but remembered so many more filled with wonderful memories. Although she didn't remember that day, it is one I will never forget because it started me on the true path to learning to teach.

I needed to *learn* how to be a good teacher. I needed to *learn* how to be a program manager. My first book, *Habits of a Successful Band Director*, grew from these experiences. Everyone gets something different from the book, but more than anything, people seem to crave the strategies. I also believe that the leadership component is critical not just for your program but for the person you become. Leadership, like band, is a process. I used to see both of them as a destination point. I don't think I was the only one who thought this way. I think that most young teachers see it this way.

> I did not learn these things in college, nor do most teachers. It is not possible for a university to teach you everything, but I also believe that the universities that really get it bring current and contemporary issues into the classroom. Young teachers fresh out of college have trouble separating friendliness with the students from their students' friends. I think they also struggle with seeing music as a profession and not just a passion. I knew how to be friendly and professional; I just had to learn how to teach, so that is where I started.

Since that day, Scott has pursued an unquenchable desire to be the best teacher he can be.

Dimostrazione: Demonstrate through your own experience. Think for yourself.

Scott is the consummate musician. As a student he was known for his lengthy practice room vigils and was always well prepared. He understands the discipline and commitment required to be successful. He understands that you have to teach from where you are and readily admits that as he grew as a person, so did his teaching.

> There are teachers who are great managers of people but not great musicians, and there are great musicians who are poor managers of people. You have to have both skill sets. I believe that you can learn to be a great teacher. I also

believe that you can constantly improve your musical artistry. Whatever your shortcomings, you can learn to be a great teacher of music.

I had a good friend and colleague call me not long ago. He had finished his tour of duty in a military band and was looking at what was next. He was a fantastic musician and was not ready to give it up completely, so he went into teaching. He called to tell me that it just wasn't working out and asked me for some help. As our conversation evolved and I began to probe about what was going on, he asked me if I liked my job. When I said Yes, he asked Why?

You have to understand that he was a great musician who was really struggling with classroom management. Musically speaking he had it all on the inside but could not get it to the outside. He could model things but could not teach them. So we began to talk about the basics of classroom management and the skill sets required to run a program. He had to learn those skills so that he could model them.

Sensazione: Sharpen your senses, the secret to enjoying life and savoring every sensation.

My life outside of band is pretty structured as well. I don't have a lot of free time, but what little

I have is spent with my family because they are important to me. They keep me focused on why I do what I do. My wife Michelle and I both make it a point to take one day each week and come home early to spend time together as a family. At school we rotate the assignments among the staff so everyone gets at least one early day each week. You need that time to refresh and stay sharp.

After Thomas, my first, was born, everything changed. You can't describe it to anyone who hasn't felt it, but it's real. Through him I have lived more and felt more than ever before. I treasure each and every moment I have with him. It has made me a better teacher and a better musician.

Scott's teaching sidekick and biggest fan, Lanie Radecke, says,

He changed as a teacher after Thomas came along. Before, he saw his students as his profession; now I think he sees a future Thomas in each and every one of them. This has endeared him more to his students and made their relationship even more important to him.

Just as he balances his role as a father and teacher, so he does as a conductor and musician. As he describes the difference between making music and playing music, he reflects on the battle between being a great technician and being artistic. To make a point he shares the story of a tense rehearsal just weeks before Wando's performance at the prestigious Midwest Clinic.

> The kids were playing well, I mean really well. We had all the notes and rhythms, and the kids were playing in tune and with a great characteristic sound. And yet we weren't making music. As a group, we had no soul, and we weren't communicating anything. I was frustrated.
>
> In order to demonstrate the difference between playing and emoting, I decided to take a chance. I asked for four volunteers from the ensemble. I put the students in order, gave them a key signature and told them they each had four measures to communicate a musical message or emotion in that key. It was almost like improv for concert band. I expected each one of the four performers to listen to what was played in the four measures prior to their entrance and build upon the message of the musician before them. When the last person was done, sixteen measures later, even I was amazed at what had just happened and the depth of their understanding. They had taken a simple four measure melody, transformed it into an emotive

theme and were able to communicate with the rest of the ensemble. We went around the room and talked about what that message was and how well they had communicated it. The ensemble never sounded the same after that.

In order to make music you have to be open to taking risks. You have to be willing to feel the sting of failure in a public venue. You have to be willing to take what's on the inside and display it for the world to see. With this heightened state of vulnerability comes a deeper understanding and feeling. When I see Scott on stage or in rehearsal, I get the feeling that he is completely in the moment.

Sfumato: Be open to the unknown and willing to embrace uncertainty.

Scott is the first to admit that teaching has changed a great deal since he began.

> More so than ever before, music education is in a state of flux. High-stakes testing and the increased demands placed on the public school system have created a climate of fear among many music educators. This culture of accountability coupled with a new generation of students have many teachers wondering what a band room will look like ten or twenty years from now.

I believe that student musicians will continue to get better and better with the passage of time. In addition to being better musicians, they will learn and think differently than the teenagers of today. Teachers need to be ready to motivate students in a way that is meaningful to them. As their world changes, so must our way of communication and motivation. Change is hard, especially when it involves something we aren't familiar with, like technology, but change is necessary to stay relevant and effective. As kids improve, so must the teachers standing in front of them. Kids are better now than they were twenty years ago because teachers are better now than they were twenty years ago; and both will continue to improve.

However, I am concerned that the model used in some universities is incomplete and does not prepare future teachers for everything that they are about to face. The universities that prepare their students for the complete classroom experience are hitting the nail on the head, and that means teaching more than pedagogy and conducting technique. Technology, for example, is about to make a significant impression on music education. We need to be ready to embrace and use these tools as they come along.

Arte/Scienza: Balance art and science, logic and imagination. Leonardo da Vinci said, "Study the science of art and the art of science."

Few people would ever guess that Scott had a passion for people that would lead him to the classroom. He is a serious and sober person with analytical skills and an intellect to match. At first glance you don't see the warm, fuzzy side of Scott that you typically see in a teacher. Nor do you see the "edu-tainer" that can captivate over a hundred of today's multitasking teenagers. But whether you see it or not, it's there. Scott understands better than most the disconnect between the engaging teacher and the program manager, and is able to meet the needs of both sides with surprising dexterity.

"The two worlds of the artist and educator have to meet," he says as a matter of fact.

> If you are a great musician, then that is something that you need to bring to the table. But if you lack the other skills needed to teach, then it just won't work. You have to be more than a great musician to be a great teacher.

Just as Scott shared his tips for success with his good friend he has done so with thousands of others. His book, *Habits of a Successful Band Director*, and its equally impressive sequel, *The Evolution of the Successful Band Director*, have sold over ten thousand copies to date and are just in their infancy. A model practitioner of the art of teaching and running a significant organization, Scott's books move with great fluency from the art of making music to the art of teaching. In *Habits of the Successful Band Director*, Scott spends the first four chapters and nearly one third of the entire book discussing the development and evolution of a director's non-teaching responsibilities.

When I asked Scott about how he balances these two very divergent roles, he explained,

> It's not that I want to be known as a great manager of people, because I don't. Some teachers just don't understand that in addition to teaching music, we are public school educators as well. You need to be perceived as a team player on your faculty and leave the cave of the band room. I am firmly convinced that the reason I was selected as *Teacher of the Year* was because I said good morning to everyone I saw and told my students to do the same thing. My philosophy is that we are in the people business first.
>
> Keep in mind that the kind of people we are is more important than the musician we become. Yes, we have booster boards, students, and administrators, and to an extent they are our customers. In that sense we are a business, but that is not all that we do. We have the opportunity to affect lives and we get to use music to do it. We could not and should not

measure our success by the number of student musicians we deal with, but by how many of them can connect with music.

Corporalità: Balance your mind and body.

Scott's façade is a serious and sober one that might be better suited to that of an accountant. He is not demonstrative and would not be described as overly charismatic. He is not particularly eloquent, and brevity of speech is not his strength. A wiry man with a slender build (all of five feet and ten inches), his hair in retreat and his mustache intact, he reminds one more of the friendly produce manager at the local grocery than the great musician he is. He is by no means a meek or meager person, but he is more reserved than you might imagine, given his history of performance and daily work with large groups of people.

Scott knows the importance of being healthy. He knows that his job can take a toll and desperately wants to be an active part of his young son's life for decades to come. He knows all of this, and yet this is where we find his Achilles heel. This is where we find a small but perceptible hole in his virtual body of armor. Yes, in this da Vincian science he fails, but as with everything else that is Scott Rush, he does so with great conviction.

His assistant director, Lanie Radecke says,

> Scott never met a chocolate chip cookie that he didn't like. They are his favorite food group.

Each day during lunch, if he doesn't have any cookies around, he sends a student to the vending machine. It's almost as if chocolate chip cookies are an extension of his being.

In the mornings, when most of us are still battling to lift our eyelids, you will find Scott at his desk with a can of soda. Last year, they changed all of the vending machines near us to diet soda and I thought he was going to throw a nutty. I mean, he was really upset. It was so funny to watch. He does make an attempt to stay healthy, albeit not a significant one. He eats those healthy microwaveable meals every day and even climbs aboard a treadmill every once in awhile, but if someone says the word dessert, you better get out of his way, as he will take no prisoners in pursuit of satisfying his sweet tooth. I am not sure how he stays so thin. I think it is just his tireless energy level.

Connessione: Realize that everything connects to everything else.

What was once considered "geek speak"—a decidedly left-brain activity—has become a component of our daily vocabulary as our society continues to value the logical, analytic skills required by advancing technology. However, Scott's success lies in his right-brain ability (associated with intuitive, spontaneous insight) to connect the product with the process to create an incredible learning environment. I suspect that this unique ability would make him successful in a corner office high above Park Avenue or as the CEO of a Fortune 500 company.

Lanie says,

> Scott Rush would make the perfect CEO. His ability to grasp all of the pieces of the puzzle is incredible to watch and even more incredible to work with. He knows how to take the administration, his staff, student leaders, and boosters and get them all on the same page. His ability to not only see the big picture but get everyone else to see it as well is something truly special to witness.

Scott says,

> You are a product of your musical experiences. As a young teacher you are a summation of the opportunities you have had as a part of your educational training. With that said, there have been some great musicians that had artistry on their instrument, but could not communicate it effectively to students. Assuming that is the case, then we have to assume that there is something more to the equation than just being a great musician. The musical experiences you share

with your students have to be ones that you have experienced yourself. If you aren't experiencing them in school, or professional development, then you have to create them for yourself. You have to find those people who can mentor you and help to provide those experiences for you. Even though I had been in successful band programs, it was not until I saw successful teachers in action that I had my light-bulb moment of what a band program could truly be. It's not the traditional model we plot in college, but a successful model nonetheless.

In that respect Scott followed the traditional model. He was a master musician who stood out as an undergraduate and eventually as a graduate student at New England Conservatory. As an adult, he participated in both sides of the process simultaneously, teaching students while taking courses to become a teacher. Having that dual experience has given him some unique insights to the teacher training process.

Our imbalanced training process has created a generation of music educators that lacks professional balance—a balance that is critical not only to running a successful and complex program but to survival in this age of increased academic and professional accountability. Has this imbalance always been there? Possibly. However, it has become more dangerous in this new era of accountability.

Times have changed for our public schools, and we as music teachers have not kept pace. Student performance once measured by the first five letters of the alphabet with added points for citizenship, behavior, and artistic penmanship is now viewed through a different and far more complex lens. The snapshot of student performance now includes scores from SAT, PSAT, ASVAB, ACT, national, state, and local tests. In addition, colleges are also considering portfolios, activities, attendance, leadership skills, after-school jobs, and so much more. Students now face a world in which their entire academic future can be altered by a mere thousandth of a point. This insatiable thirst for data has music education, an art form that struggles to defy definition by data-driven standards, relegated to a second tier status.

So what is wrong with this? What's wrong with accountability? What's wrong with data? The answer is *Nothing*. As music teachers we use ratings, scores, rankings, and musical rubrics to help develop better student performance. We use data and assessment all the time to improve the art of what we do. Our festivals use rubrics. Audition music is adjudicated on precise metronomic and dynamic markings. We give playing tests and employ professional evaluators. We have even developed electronic tools such as SmartMusic™ that help us more clinically identify and correct performance shortcomings.

This is where art meets science and the right brain embraces the left in an attempt to increase student learning. With increasing frequency our profession and our world will call upon the whole-brain thinker: the person who understands both the artistic and the analytical sides and can marry the two. When we use our whole brain we are more likely to be teaching the whole child, but drawing the line between the two is difficult. As Scott Rush says,

> I believe that auditions and evaluation music are a normal part of the process of being a musician. There are auditions for every major orchestral or professional band job, there are auditions into colleges, and auditions for scholarships, summer festivals, etc. It is a necessary part of what we do and I have no problem with auditions being used in this manner. I also don't have a problem with teaching students how to be most effective in the evaluation process. There are colleges that now offer classes and summer workshops on how to maximize your audition success, almost like classes on how to better SAT scores.
>
> *However*, I *do* have a problem with people who get caught up in what rating they must receive at festival or what score they should get at a marching contest. I've even seen situations where administrators have used ratings or scores to determine a director's worth (i.e., whether she should keep her job). And I absolutely have a problem with parents who determine their child's self-worth based on whether he makes first chair in the audition.

This is where the whole-brain thinker has to synthesize all of this information and create a learning environment that meets the needs of the student and teaches process as well as performance. All are important and are requisite for true success. We need the scholar to teach the student. We need academics to advance the arts. We need process to create a product. We need individuals to create an ensemble. We need both sides of the brain to make a successful program and successful experiences for kids.

Scott says,

> When a band plays at the Midwest Clinic, they don't get a score, rating, or adjudication tapes. Instead, they are a part of an extraordinary experience of music making, both from the standpoint of the people who are involved (i.e., guest conductors) and the chance to play for one of the most appreciative audiences in the world. At its highest level, what we do is about interpreting ink on a page and communicating through the language of music, one soul to another.

Great ensembles and great teachers have to balance the two: technical mastery and artistic integrity. Great programs have a balance between high musical standards and an organization that supports it. One without the other is short-term success doomed for long-term failure.

Scott says,

> When I ended up at Wando High School, I followed a younger but equally successful teacher. He had developed the program from mediocrity to a place of accomplishment. The kids were successful and were not excited to see him leave. They didn't see any reason for change. I needed to show them that I had a plan, that I was not their friend, but someone who had something to offer them. I remember one senior coming in to complain about some decisions I had made. I reminded him that he was on the seven-month plan while I was on the seven-year plan.

And true to his word, seven years after that conversation, Scott published his first book to rave reviews, saw his band selected to perform at the Midwest Clinic, and accepted the Sudler Flag of Honor for his program. Success such as this is a manifestation of both musical and organizational diligence and effort. I believe that Scott used the plan of seven: seven years and seven sciences. Like everything else he says, when he said seven years, he wasn't just making it up, he was making a plan.

The balance between the art of making music and the process of building a program has left many an unsuccessful teacher it its wake. There is no way to separate one from the other, and our abilities as coordinators continue to evolve alongside the increasing demands of being a classroom educator. Scott established his musical prowess through years of hard work and extensive training. He learned his process from his first teaching job and working along side his classroom mentor, Ms. Lorraine Paris.

> Lorraine had been a music teacher in town for forty-seven years. When I was hired, she ran the high school and I ran the middle school and assisted one period a day. I took a twelve thousand dollar pay cut to come work with her and it was worth every penny. I learned more about the people business from her than anyone else I have ever met. She wasn't just a music teacher in that community, she *was* the community. It wasn't what she taught, but how she taught it that made her so magical.
>
> She would never conduct the *Hounds of Spring* or *Lincolnshire Posy* in her career, but she transformed an entire generation of kids and was revered by her community. I may have had a more extensive background in music, but she knew more about people. She was an artist in a way that I knew nothing about.

Teaching music is as much a left-brained vocation as a right brained avocation and should be treated as such. As music teachers we are so wrapped up in the emotional connection we have with our profession and our students that we see ourselves as musicians more than teachers. We see teaching band as an extension or continuation of our being in band. We see ourselves as conductors more than program managers. We see things more comfortably through the right side of our brain while continually working in a left-brained world. Scott Rush puts it best when he says,

> I think the *great* programs have figured out how to balance the artistry of making music and the rigidity of running a large organization. Ten years ago I thought I had it figured out. I was not a new teacher, but I was not an old one, either. Now I *know* that I don't have it figured it out; but I *do* have a strong sense of how to get things better. I do this by putting structure into the program. You have to get to a point where you can make great music and concurrently run a great organization. You have to be artistic in every sense.
>
> In addition to music, I see artistry in running a program.

Scott just might be the da Vinci of our profession, if he could just put that chocolate chip cookie down. But don't tell him you know about his obsession... he thinks it's a secret.

Chapter Seven

The Dynamics of Life

*On maintaining perspective with
Diana Williams of Webb City High School*

"I remember the phone call like it was yesterday," Diana says with calmness.

Sitting in the lobby of the Chicago Hilton and Towers in a grey two-piece suit with her hair pulled back, onlookers would think Diana to be a sharp and savvy businesswoman instead of the high school band director that she is. In this plush but cold setting, surrounded by strangers, it almost felt as if she and I were talking about something mundane or common, as though we were discussing the weather or politics or our favorite composer... but we weren't. We were talking about a day that changed Diana's family and her life, forever.

As she recounted the horrific events of that day, she remains polished and professional beyond reproach. The words came out of her mouth and I marveled at her poise and control. Given the nature of our conversation and the ordeal that she had been through, I doubt that I would have been able to do the same. Her voice inflection and demeanor gave no indication that she was recounting the most difficult eight months of her life; months which changed her and her family forever; months that she never would ask for, but that she doesn't regret.

At first glance that day was like any other, fast-paced rehearsals and faster-paced lunches. Diana and her assistant, Valeska, worked through lunch as usual, gobbling down food while trying to make a dent in the growing mound of paperwork. That day was one of those days. As with all band directors, there was too much to do and not enough time to do it. Multitasking, the ladies could fill out requisitions, respond to emails, and answer the phone while eating half a sandwich and drinking a Diet Coke. Then the phone rang. Assuming it was a call from a colleague or a question from her booster president, Diana reached to answer it, mouth half full of food.

> I paused before I picked it up. On the other line was Sarah, our good friend and wife of my husband Wade's boss. Over the years our two families had become very close friends and it was not unusual for her to call. Not normal, but not unusual. I could immediately tell something was wrong by the tone in her voice, but before I could ask her what it was, Sarah blurted, "Wade has been in an accident."
>
> The words rang in my ears but did not fully register in my mind. My head and heart raced to play catch-up as I tried to understand and

process what she was saying. Not knowing the severity of the situation, but knowing how tough my husband is, I was able to remain calm. Part of having an active husband and a teenage son meant dealing with broken bones and the occasional set of stitches. To try and get a feel of how bad the situation was, I asked if he was okay.

Sarah paused for a moment and said, "Diana, they're doing everything they can." That's when I knew he had been seriously hurt.

As Diana described the accident, she did so with unimaginable poise.

Wade had been doing work in the construction industry for a while. He was between jobs when our friend Neil, a roofing contractor, asked him to come work with him on some upcoming projects. Wanting to help his friend, Wade agreed. A few months into his new job Wade was walking along a roof when he fell through a hole that was covered only with insulation and had no support materials below. There was no way he could have seen this gap and he was completely unaware of it. This left a two hundred and ten pound man plunging toward the ground with only fiberglass insulation as his buffer.

Upon hitting the ground Wade struck his head with significant force and was left unconscious and unresponsive.

I asked Diana to return to the phone call and tell me what happened next.

In the whirlwind of the moment, as I was processing all of this information, somewhere in the back of my mind my thoughts went to Neil, my husband's boss, as he had recently recovered from a similar fall. I took some small comfort in the fact that he had survived. I believed that if he could recover from his fall, I knew my husband would as well. I was scared, but I was about to get even more scared.

Diana asked Sarah, "Who is with Wade now?" "One of his co-workers..." Sarah answered. "They are bringing in a medivac chopper."

With those seven words, I was jolted into the reality that he wasn't just seriously hurt, he was fighting for his life. I immediately hung up the phone and turned to my co-worker, Valeska, to tell her what had happened. She grabbed her keys and drove me to the hospital. As we ran out of the office, I looked back to my TA and said, "Tell everyone that all after-school activities are cancelled."

And then they raced out the door.

When Diana arrived at the hospital, she was briefed on what had happened. At that moment she did not care what had happened or how it happened; she only cared about where her husband was and wanted to know how he was doing. Everything else could wait.

Later, surrounded by family and friends, Diana met with the doctors and received word of his condition. Traumatic brain injury, along with other superficial wounds, with no real prognosis of how this would end. Wade was in a coma—a deep sleep that he could possibly emerge from, with the outcome unknown until he woke up. Even worse, he might never wake up. At that point, the enormity and seriousness of his condition began to wash over Diana. For the first time she understood that his recovery would not just be the seven months he would eventually spend in and out of care facilities, but that it would last a lifetime.

> To look at him now, you wouldn't know how life-threatening Wade's situation was. There was a period of time when we didn't know if he would recover and what long-term damage he might have sustained, but in the following months he surprised everyone and made significant progress. Despite the extensive ground Wade

has covered, the effects of such a serious fall are life-altering and have forever changed him.

Prior to the accident, Diana was a person who possessed an almost singular focus. She loved her job and enjoyed applying her endless supply of energy to it. Even after more than a decade, she loved her career and relished the sense of purpose it had given her life. As a professional, her obstacles were great but her resolve was greater. She knew what needed to be done and was not shy about rolling up her sleeves and doing it herself. She had found her place in this world and reveled in both its comforts and challenges. In addition to being a band director, Diana was a wife and mother, and she pursued both with equal fervor. With her son in band and her husband a fellow band geek, the lines between home and work were blurred; but she had learned to walk that tightrope with the deft and dexterity of a veteran circus performer.

A self-described driven person, Diana has always had a passion for success in life. She knew from a very young age that she wanted to be a music educator and pursued her dream with relentless energy. A petite woman in her early forties with striking features, she is a driven educator who will go to great lengths to see her students and her program succeed. Professional to a fault, with a poker face that would be the envy of Las Vegas, she is all business and is not shy about taking command of the classroom or a situation. Known for her calm under pressure and presence on the podium, she is well liked and respected by her students and colleagues.

Webb City is a small and charming rural town on the border between Missouri and Oklahoma. Without the advantages of even a moderately sized city, this bedroom community lacks many of the amenities one typically associates with a successful school and band program. Webb City does not boast a large student enrollment, abundant financial resources, strong business community support, or even a nearby university. There are no nearby music stores or private lesson teachers. Yet the program had reached a modicum of success. The band has appeared in numerous local, regional, and national events, including the Tournament of Roses Parade and has been active in the Missouri band circuit. Given the circumstances, some might consider the program an anomaly of sorts, but the school and the band program are a source of pride for this small and sometimes struggling community.

Diana has lived within a hundred miles of Webb City her entire life. She met her husband, went to college, and raised her son in the same small-town environment where they grew up. After a decade of teaching at Webb, she understood her school and recognized the culture and rural environment to be both comforting and frustrating. She loved the close-knit ways of her community, but knew that it also inhibited the students' growth. The community and students wanted to be successful, but their lack of exposure to other groups and national trends had placed a false ceiling above the band. The community had long supported the music program, but only in that it served as a source of entertainment and civic pride. Prior to Diana's arrival the band had enjoyed the occasional regional event, but focused more on local and state events and communal parades than competing on a regional or national level.

The pursuit of success however, came at a price.

> I would get to work by seven AM and would very often still be there being doing sectionals or rehearsing a band or group until seven, eight, or nine PM. I was willing to do what needed to be done, whenever it needed to be done. To me it wasn't a big deal; it was the price you paid. I was happy, not content, but happy. It seemed that no matter how hard I worked, there was more to be done. I felt like I was always chasing my tail. My son Devon was in the band, so he understood, and Wade was as supportive as a husband can be. He cooked every night while I worked. This was just the way it was and it worked for us.

She pauses.

> I will be the first to admit that my family came second and my job came first.

As the words came out of her mouth, you could hear the regret in her voice. She knew that there was nothing she could do to change the past, but she also knew she could learn from it. She is not alone in her regret. She is certainly not the first band director to utter those words or have these thoughts. It seems almost systemic in our profession and universal among our colleagues, but her regret is magnified by her situation. She shares her cautionary tale with hopes of reminding others not to ignore what they have and to put first things first. Her courage in sharing it with me shows her to be a giant of a person.

There are no equals in education when it comes to the cross-pollination of personal and professional lives. As a rule, music teachers are among the first to arrive at school and the last to go home. While their colleagues are running for the parking lot, music teachers are running to their next rehearsal. While other teachers are screaming for smaller classes, music teachers want to recruit more kids. Our nights and weekends are defined not by our personal passions but by honor bands and contests. In our "spare time," we attend concerts, conventions, and drum corps shows. When we watch sporting events on TV, we use the restroom during the game to not miss the halftime coverage. We critique the National Anthem more than the starting line-up and watch the crowd shots in hopes of catching a glimpse of the band. By default, self-preservation, or shared passions, many of our friends are also our colleagues. This blending of work and non-work creates the opportunity for a lifestyle that lacks balance and objectivity. We must live in the world we create, but the tightrope walk between our two worlds can strip us of a healthy and appropriate perspective on music education and its role in our students' lives.

Teaching is as much an avocation as a vocation, and in order to be successful, both components need to be present. The difficulty lies in finding the right balance and maintaining it. As time and life circumstances change, so should we.

* * *

As a general rule, our educational colleagues are better able to separate what is professional and what is personal. This is not an indictment, but an observation of how we have come to define ourselves. I don't see math teachers studying batting averages during baseball games. I don't overhear English teachers talking about taking personal sick days for professional use and paying their own way to conferences. I have never heard of a history teacher taking her students to history camp two weeks before school. I don't see it, hear it, or experience it, because, by and large, it is not happening. Most teachers see their lives outside of teaching as an experience and not an in-service.

In music education we sometimes struggle to tell the difference between a vocation and a vacation. This obsessive behavior is growing more prevalent, and it colors our judgment and alters the way we teach music. As the demands required for success rise, so does what's required of us. While some see this as negative, it is in fact one of our greatest assets. We are so personally invested in our profession that it is often hard to separate the two. But separation of powers might be just what is necessary to keep our profession and ourselves in proper perspective.

I asked Diana why she was willing to be part of this book and share something so personal and painful.

> I am not sure why things happen, but I know they happen for a reason. Maybe by sharing our struggles we can help someone else grow. I am not sure what my role is, but I know there is a role.

Being the consummate educator that she is, I asked her what she would want to teach to other music teachers. She paused.

> The job is not the core of who you are. Your band does not define you. No one is going to put my job title on my gravestone. It won't list the accolades and awards that we have achieved because that is not who I am. My tombstone will read Wife and Mother, because that is who I am. This is the most important contest I will ever go to. This is the most important rating I will ever receive. With Wade's recovery, we are living day to day, and for now, that is enough. We still have some significant issues to deal with and a lifetime of recovery ahead of us. This is how I am judged now, and there is no rubric for that.

And with that, she brings up a key point in the discussion of how we as music teachers got to this point, and asks, Where do we go from here? Through our desire to quantify excellence and establish standards of performance, we have created a culture that rewards the product and not the process. It rewards performance over personal and musical growth, and as we all know, what gets rewarded gets repeated. This is not a condemnation of our profession, but more of a question. Simply stated, Where is the balance between process and product and what we are trying to achieve? In many ways, the struggle between the personal and professional mirrors the struggle between our process and product. What is the correlation here? If we were able to quantify the values first, prior to establishing our systems, would our profession look very different? Not better, but different?

For example, what if at contest:

- Instead rewarding the highest score, we rewarded the greatest differential or growth factor from the prior week or previous season?
- We factored in average age of the students, private lessons, or level of honor band participation?
- We factored in the number of ensemble offerings at the school?
- We factored in the number of directors or staff members? We factored in the socioeconomic status of the students?
- We factored in the experience level of the director?

Presumably we value all of these things, and yet they are not present in our evaluative tools. We live in a world that places a premium on quantitative data, but to ignore the fact that such data often stands in the way of true learning and measurable growth merely serves to continue the practice. There is no arguing that the process determines the product, but equally true is the fact that the product determines the process. Which is more important? Which comes first?

Whether it is to satisfy our competitive drive or address the insatiable need for personal and professional validation, we have created a system that qualifies and quantifies success for our students and ourselves as based almost exclusively on the end product. Are we providing better musical experiences? Or have we stepped into professional quicksand which is swallowing music education in lieu of music performance?

What do you think? Your answer might not only reflect your views, but where and what age level you teach. At one time, universities ensembles were performance-based and focused on professional preparation and stretching the bounds of musical artistry. The role of the secondary setting was establishing an understanding of the ensemble concepts required to be successful in a more advanced or collegiate setting. Finally, the role of the elementary school was to establish the foundation and fundamentals required for successful participation in musical ensembles.

Now, successful high school programs more resemble their collegiate counterparts as they close the gap between artistry and achievement. However, this performance-based approach can leave students without some primary music skill sets unless they study privately. If you were to survey band programs around the country, I believe you would find substantial evidence that our changing approach to music education has simultaneously elevated performing ensembles to greater heights than ever before while leaving the music knowledge of individual students at historical lows. Our pursuit of the flawless ensemble has left us with flawed performers. Last year's collegiate premier is this year's honor band piece. This year's wind band commission is next year's contest piece. The gap between the artistry of drum corps and the achievement of Bands of America is shrinking. This is not the case in other classrooms. The bar for algebra remains as it was decades ago, and in many cases has been lowered. The study of Shakespeare's works has seen little change since its introduction into our curricula.

The demands of our profession have accelerated since I started teaching. In fact, with each year it seems to grow almost exponentially. We have added so much in the past decade that if we continue at this pace, music education could crash and burn. We need to stop and regroup and decide what is most important. Take our winter programs for example. I see them as valuable components to students' experiences, but not at the cost of other groups, such as jazz or percussion ensembles.

Diana says,

> This is not just an issue for us as teachers; it is an issue for our students as well. At our high school

we have concurrent offerings for students in seven different areas: concert band(s), jazz band, winter guard, percussion ensemble, woodwind/brass ensemble, pep band, and winter drum line. And it is the same kids making it all happen. I am not sure who is more likely to burn out, the kids or us as teachers.

The gap between artistry and achievement is more elusive than ever, but has it come at a cost? Does the end justify the means? In many music rooms drill and repetition have replaced scope and sequence. Passion for performance has exceeded passion for the music. Numbers and scores instead of appreciation and artistry are the measure of achievement. As music educators, we join our colleagues in rebelling against teaching to the test and objectives of standardized assessment. Yet we remain standard bearers for implementation of these as we champion the cause of assessment-based education. When we place students in ability-based ensembles, we are in fact tracking our students. When we choose the "right" program for contest, we are differentiating instruction. When we spend ninety-eight percent of our rehearsal time in preparation for a festival or contest, we are teaching to the test.

Whether we like it or not, predominant in the music education profession is the very system being championed by policy makers and pundits alike. By teaching to the festival rubric, are we not teaching to the test? By choosing from required literature are we not limiting what students can experience? The question is, Did we do it by decision or by default? Band directors celebrate their successes and survive their failures all in the glaring eye of the public, and are seen almost single-handedly as the source of all that happens within their sphere of control. We are, so often, the sole source of musical information and the onlyr is caught in the most improbable of conundrums: the need to be the master of all trades and jack of none.

In education we do not expect each and every math teacher to be equally adept in Calculus 2 as they are in Geometry. We do not expect every art teacher to be equally skilled in acrylics as they are at the pottery wheel. We do not expect each history teacher to be equally knowledgeable about the Greco-Roman era as they are with modern macroeconomics. Granted, we do not expect our music teachers to be equally proficient at all instruments, but we do hold them accountable for all students being successful on their instrument. This is not the case in other curricular areas. If it were, we would need to remove the majority of math teachers in America from their roles as teachers.

No one in her right mind would view education in such a myopic way, and yet this is not such a far-fetched exaggeration of the situation we have created in our profession. The typical band director is expected to be equally adept in the idioms of marching, concert, and jazz. Band directors are expected within these areas to have equal understanding and proficiency on every woodwind, brass, and percussion instrument, as they are often the sole instructional provider. Music teachers are expected to achieve the same level of success at contest with freshman as they are their seniors, and when we are finished with our expert analysis of the job they have done, we publish it for one and all to see as an indicator of their success.

I doubt that this scenario is something new to music education. I venture to guess that teachers long before you and I have struggled for decades with these very same issues; but I do believe it has become magnified in recent years. Regardless of the reason, the days of eight-to-four with weekends and summers off are all but gone for music teachers. This does not mean that past generations were not comprised of passionate and committed professionals who pushed for excellence. The desire to communicate to young people the importance and the value of music and the process by which we learn it is something that predates Mozart himself. The story of the maddening and tyrannical teacher inspiring the young artist is as well documented as any in the cultural lore of music. What has changed is the complexity of the music education landscape and the dynamic of how we view student achievement. In short, what has changed is our perspective.

Typically, perspective is something that comes after the fact, something most obvious when viewed in retrospect. We see mistakes after they have been made. We see wisdom after suffering the ramifications. We feel love more deeply after the person is gone. Professionally speaking, it is no different. We have a greater sense of clarity after we achieve closure. The rating feels different after the festival. The performance sounds different on CD that it did on stage. With time, the music will fade from memory more quickly than the vision of the students who performed it. Our students mean more to us after they are gone. It is as if our rearview mirror has greater visibility than our windshield, or at least has something better to look at. Rather than see our ensembles for all that *they* could and should be, we see them as a vehicle for what we could and should be.

We are hanging on for dear life, living from event to event, hoping to get that next hit from the audience, to get that next "aha" moment from a student. This educational high is our drug of choice. In these moments we are in search of a higher high, which is often followed by lower lows. In the pursuit of success we push a little harder, work a little later, start a little earlier, and rehearse a little longer, all in hope of finding another one of those moments. We want success, both for our students and ourselves. The desire for success is a part of the human condition, but from the outside looking in, many of us have become success junkies looking for our next trophy fix.

Diana states,

> I've never cared what other directors thought or what was popular. I have always been able to separate what I wanted to achieve as a director and what was best for my students. I want my students to be aware of what is current and what

> is possible in the art form, but I want to make choices for them based on what is appropriate and not popular.

Even inside the profession, we are often almost predatory in defense of our own shortcomings; and anyone who has been judged by their peers or performed at a music conference knows it. Those who should be the most supportive tend to be the most critical. We are collegial by choice and critical by nature, and oftentimes we are left to our own devices when looking for ways to improve and grow. Given the isolation and all that our jobs encompass, it is no wonder that less than fifty percent of all teachers last more than five years. When you also factor in the amount of people who burn out in music schools all across this country, you can see a disturbing trend.

Diana says,

> I remember listening to the veteran directors at meetings and conferences and learning from them. Today's younger teachers seem to have more confidence, which is good to a point, but I think inhibits their professional growth. If we want *all* programs to be successful, we are going to have to bridge that gap or we all are going to pay the price. They will burn out at a much faster rate—and we cannot fill that gap if the teachers simply aren't there. Mentoring is *vital* to the growth of music education.

This clarity and conviction which comes from perspective does not end at the rehearsal room door, but they can help you to survive and thrive in almost any situation. I am far removed from the day-to-day struggles that most of you face, and I have never been associated with the daily challenges that Diana faces, but I can still learn from her. Through her experiences I am afforded the luxury of her wisdom and perspective. I am completely disassociated with virtually every aspect of her life, and yet with her help, my vision is growing clearer. I am not 20/20 yet, but I am seeing more and more through her lens.

Diana says,

> I believe that every kid can learn to play and love music. Prior to the accident I think that it was harder for me to understand students who didn't seem committed or appeared to be lost within the program. Now I find myself working harder to reach out to every student. I am working harder to make sure that everyone can be vested in some part of our program.

Diana has learned this from her husband, but she has also learned how to be a better spouse from her job. In one of Diana's final postings on the blog she created to keep family and friends in the know during her husband's recovery process, she reflects on the struggles that lay before her both as a wife and a teacher. As you read her thoughts you can see her philosophy of teaching changing as she reflects on the journey that lays ahead of her now. She writes:

> We leave in two weeks for Denver and head back to Craig for Wade's first evaluation since we left in June. I must tell you that we are *very* excited about going back! We really miss it there. We really enjoyed the people and the atmosphere. We miss the push to get back to life, and we really miss the I-can-do attitude from the therapists that pushed him. We do have one therapist here who I totally have faith in and is doing a wonderful job. But, sadly, the other two have told Wade that "This is the best it will be..." or "I can't do anymore for you." What a letdown.
>
> What if I did that as a teacher? What if I looked a parent in the eyes and said, "I can't do anymore for your child. This is the best he will ever get." This totally would not fly. Nor would I even begin to think of doing such a thing! If I run out of things to do to reach a student... *I look for more answers or find someone who can*! But not in this situation. We are left here to slog through and look for someone else. We are not giving up, nor are we going to give in. Every day is a new day, a day that God has made, and one that I know He has given us

to continue to glorify Him. I know that Wade will be healed. I am waiting to go to Craig to get our next course of action.

Diana truly has a unique and admirable perspective, both as an educator and as a person. She seems to see the big things for what they are and the little things for what they aren't, and I can't help but think it makes her a better teacher and a better person.

At the time of this writing it has not yet been a year since Wade fell, and yet so much has changed even as so much remains the same. There are still sectionals to be held, emails to respond to, purchase orders to be filled out, and contests to attend. Diana's role as a program coordinator is larger than ever and growing every day. Her roles as a wife, mother, and care provider are growing at an even faster rate. She operates with a great deal of efficiency and in a business-like manner both in and out of the classroom. She understands the enormity of her responsibility and that she is only one person. Diana lives in the moment and gives each task her full attention, but can also see its relevance in the greater picture of her life. Part as coping mechanism and part out of necessity, she does this all in hopes of keeping all of the balls she is juggling safely in the air for as long as possible. I believe that she knows that eventually one of the balls will come crashing down, and she takes a great deal of solace in knowing that her colleagues and student leaders will be there to pick it up and toss it back in the air when she is ready.

> I have always known who I was and what I wanted, but after the accident, I knew I wanted it to be different, to be better than it was before, but I didn't know how to get it there.

These are powerful words coming from someone who likes controlling all of the strings to ensure that the end result meets her standards and is reflective of her vision. In this way, she is no different than most of us. Call it controlling, call it micromanaging, or call it being a good teacher; we thrive on not only creating the vision but also seeing it through to its fruition. Maybe fueled partly by necessity and partly by desire, Diana has had to let go of some things she might be more comfortable holding on to. She has had to let some things go undone that she would rather see done. She has had to rely on her colleagues and students more than she ever did before. She has had to have faith in others that where she stops, they will start, and that through this they are learning and leading as well as helping. Through this, her students are not being served less but being served more.

Diana is a deeply religious person. She is a devout believer in a higher power and greater sense of purpose. She is always quick to give praise to God and trusts that there is a greater plan to her life. She believes that she is where she is supposed to be and is doing what she is supposed to be doing. She has faith in herself as a professional and understands her imperfections are a part of not just her growth but her students' growth as well. She has made mistakes and will continue to do so; however, she will also work to overcome them. She is tolerant and forgiving as much as she is demanding and unrelenting, and yet, with all of that faith and trust, prior to the accident, she struggled to give up control to those around her. Diana was not fully accepting of the fact that in her absence, those around her would rise to fill the void, that they would grow through her as she has grown through her experience, and that through her tragedy would come triumph, through her pain would come joy and learning, and through her brief leave from the teaching world would come a great deal of learning, that this learning might perhaps be something greater than she herself could ever teach.

Michael, Diana's assistant, had Wade's support as he helped his brother, Neil, work through his recovery process. Now Michael is standing with Wade and Diana as they struggle with similar circumstances. The circumstances which brought them together a decade ago bear no resemblance to where their relationship stands today. Beyond co-directors, they are family—if not in name, then in a more important way. When asked how Diana has changed since the accident, Michael responds:

> She has let go. She doesn't sweat the small stuff as much. She is less controlling and more open now. We have been through this twice now, once with my brother and now with Wade, and through it all, we have learned to teach with more passion and compassion. Teaching

a kid that even though it is a whole note, it is important and has something to say and communicates something to the audience. A whole note can shape a life. We talk about what the audience will say when we are done. We want to communicate what we feel in hopes that the audience will feel it as well.

When I asked how they would know if they were successful in doing that and how they could measure it, Diana responded,

> We already are, more than ever before. The kids love to play and love music. Beyond that, they have been so supportive since the accident, not just to me but also to each other. They are always there, asking if there is something that needs to be done. The student leaders are more engaged and have taken more ownership for the program. Because we are not always there, they have had to pick up the slack. You have to remember, they knew Wade too, from band trips and Friday nights. He was the jokester, the life of the party. Every year he would pick one freshman to befriend, make fun of, and goof off with, and he would stick with him until he graduated. The kids, too, lost something the day Wade fell.

Michael added,

> The accident has made us more of a family. There are always kids in the band room, hanging out and spending time together. Before, we had a goal and objective each day and that is what we did. But now, the classes are different. The students talk more about their feelings and we listen more.

Diana chimed in,

> I am more fully aware of what they are saying, not just how they are playing. My relationship with the kids is so much better than it was before. The band room just feels different. The seniors are more caring towards the freshman and the band is more caring in general.
>
> Musically speaking, I think that they understand music better now. As directors we tell students about music because they can't understand it themselves, because they have not experienced the power of it. I think that through this they have seen the power. The other day we were playing, and this musical moment was so powerful you could feel it in the room. When we stopped, you could just see on the faces of the students that they had felt something. It was amazing!

I do not know what I would do if I were in Diana's shoes, but given her strength of conviction and the depth of her perspective, I can only hope that if faced with it, I will see things as clearly as she does.

> The day of the accident I was still thinking like a band director. The staff met at the hospital and I started to list things off that needed to be done, right there outside the ER where Wade was laying and fighting for his life. That was the last time I thought like a director first.

Diana returned only once during the remaining days of the semester. She came back to conduct her wind ensemble at contest. When I asked what that was like, she responded, "The group played well." And with that answer, the old Diana emerged, the Diana Williams that is Director of Bands.

I reminded her that I did not ask how the group played; I asked what that was like. The sliding scale of perspective had momentarily been moved. But like her students, she is still a work in progress as she tries to find the fulcrum between who she is and what she does. It shows that in all things, both professional and personal, the fight for perspective and balance is going as long as we are breathing. In order to maintain perspective we have to be able to remove ourselves from a situation and see it from the outside. But in order to do so we have to understand that there has to *be* an outside.

There has to be something other than just being a Director of Bands. There has to be something other than teaching music. There has to be something more than being a caregiver. Diana reminds us that perhaps we can be more successful at many things by not focusing so much on just one thing and that balance provides a strong foundation for success.

"I had an epiphany the other day," Diana says as we begin to gather our belongings and bring our time together to a close.

> I was standing in front of the mirror, getting ready for work, reflecting on how much our lives have changed in the past eight months and it hit me. It was a clarion moment. I realized that when my time here on earth is done and I am standing in front of my maker, I will be judged on the same things that my bands have been judged on: balance, tone, and articulation. Did my life have balance? What was the tone of my time here? Was I able to clearly articulate what I believe and the feelings I have inside? I am convinced that as a person, prior to the accident, I would have received a "three" or "good" rating. A three is good, mind you, but hardly something I would accept for my students, and certainly not something I would allow for myself.

And with that single statement, Diana had come full circle. Just as she had after every festival, she took stock of her performance and went to work on making it right.

> As a family, we're a lot closer now. I don't regret what happened and I'm not bitter. I feel more balanced internally now, but I am still chasing my tail at work.

As any good director and good person will tell you, balance, blend, and articulation are always a constant struggle, both on the podium and in our lives. The problem is that as a band director at heart, Diana just won't settle for a "good."

If you would like to read Diana's online journal regarding her experiences you can do so by visiting http://www.caringbridge.org/visit/wadewilliams.

Chapter Eight

GLORIA STEINEM PASSES THE BATON

On dealing with change with Jo Ann Hood of John Overton High School

In the 230 years since the United States of America was born, few times have proven to be more tumultuous and traumatic than the early part of the 1970s. A polarizing president, Richard Nixon, was in the midst of the Watergate scandal and faced unparalleled civil unrest as the nation tried to extricate itself from the war in Vietnam. The country's wounds from a decade of civil rights riots had not healed, and recent traumatic events such as the killings at Kent State and the attempt on the life of presidential candidate George Wallace left Americans scared and uncertain about what lay ahead. Abroad, the US was dealing with an escalating arms race, an emerging giant in China, and the Olympic massacre in Munich as well as oil prices that were out of control. In American history there have been times of greater importance, but other than the Civil War, there are none in which the country was so divided and so distrustful of its leaders.

As civil unrest, high unemployment, and a faltering economy came to bear, violent clashes coupled with a distrusting public made it a difficult time for every authority figure. This problem was exponentially more difficult for those who worked with young people. The classrooms of the 1950s and early 1960s, once filled with docile and placated students, gave way to a generation of young people quick to question and slow to believe. Personal freedoms were at the forefront of the national agenda, and for the first time since the women's suffrage movement, minority status became a protected class under the law. Through it all, the largest class of people in America—women—wondered why they were not afforded similar status.

At the forefront of the women's movement was Gloria Steinem, a highly dynamic and fearless woman, and a divisive magazine publisher who was an outspoken critic of the male-dominated world. Through her powerful position as an editor and as an iconic figure, she became the spokesperson of this growing movement and an increasingly frustrated portion of America's female population. Feminists worshiped her, traditionalists despised her, and regardless of where one stood, everyone knew of and had an opinion about Gloria Steinem. But she was no Jo Ann Hood. After all, while Steinem was clamoring for equal rights, Jo Ann Hood was living it.

* * *

In the early 1970s, the field of secondary music education was a male-dominated field. Steeped in the culture of military music, bands, and more specifically, marching bands, were still deeply entrenched in their old school ways. As a part of this military heritage, women were not seen as equals and were hardly looked upon as leaders. This is not to say that there weren't successful female directors, but that they were far from the majority and not considered the norm. In the environment of the 1970s, fear was a teaching tool, and a booming voice and intimidating physical presence were considered classroom management staples. The iron fist ruled, and on any given day an ensemble could face hurling expletives or hurling objects, depending the mood of the director. It would not be much of a stretch to compare the average director with the average dictator. Sure, directors didn't kill people, but if looks could kill—well, let's just say there would be far fewer drummers in this world.

This is not to say that women were not welcome in the profession; but the unspoken belief was that women were better suited for elementary schools and choir. These people had never met someone like Jo Ann Hood. While Jo Ann was certainly all woman, she could stand toe to toe with any man, bark with the best, and drink with the worst of them. She was quick to stand up for what she believed and willing to sit down to work it out with those who disagreed. More than the legendary director of the John Overton High School Band, she is the charter female inductee into the Tennessee music teachers' Good Ole Boys Club. That was thirty years ago, and the only thing that has changed is that she is not only allowed through the gates, but is now the gatekeeper.

By any definition, Jo Ann's tenure at Overton High School has been an unqualified success. Her office and the band room are a visual cacophony of wood, plastic, and well-worn memorabilia. At first glance you might not think you were in a band room, but the back room of a very large trophy shop—one that has gone untouched for decades. It is hard to imagine one program, let alone one person, having amassed so many accolades and accomplishments. Almost lost in the memorabilia are WGI World Championships, band championships, and Sudler Flags. The proof of greatness is everywhere: on the walls, in the cabinets, on the floor, and everywhere else you look. The room is overflowing with evidence of several generations of young people meeting with success. What some see as chaos Jo Ann sees as history, perfectly staged and placed exactly as it should be, each piece having significance in and of itself but also as a piece to a much larger puzzle. She alone knows the history of the organization and serves up a daily reminder of its past in hopes that others will appreciate and embrace it as much as she does.

Her memory and her love of all things band-related is legendary among Tennessee music teachers. After all, more so than almost any person in the state she has lived it, led it, and fought to be a part of that history. There are few if any teachers in Tennessee she has not competed with, worked alongside, or drank with. And if there are any, it is their own damn fault. Since 1972 Jo Ann Hood has been a part of the fabric of music education—not just in Tennessee, but on a national level.

I remember my first concert festival like it was yesterday. I wasn't sure what to wear. That was before the days of women wearing pantsuits and it's not like there were a lot of other women band directors I could call for advice. I have to admit, I was scared to death, not of what to wear, but what to do. Just prior to my first contest, my principal scheduled a meeting and told me that if I couldn't get the job done, I wasn't gonna be gettin' tenure. Partially out of combativeness but more out of confidence, I remember telling him that I wouldn't need tenure, because if I couldn't get the job done, I wasn't going to teach!

These were brash and bold words, but words that fit Jo Ann well.

Jo Ann had few if any role models to mimic. In her childhood, there was no Take Your Daughter to Work Day (an event created by Gloria Steinem), and even if there had been, there were no female band directors within a day's drive. Whether out of necessity or opportunity, Jo Ann was forced to not only create and follow her own path, but to figure out how to survive and thrive in a male-dominated world.

Neither of my parents attended college. They were raised in a small town and were happy to be there. They never ventured far from home and were content to spend the rest of their lives that way. I would probably have done the same thing, but the local college didn't have a band program and band was all I wanted to do, so I packed my bags and left.

People always ask me what it was like to be a female band director back then. It is hard to explain, but to me, I wasn't a female band director, I was a band director who happened to be female. Success is the same whether you are wearing a blouse or a button-down shirt.

In 1972 her hair was long and her patience was short. She was demanding of her students and had little time for those who stood between her and success. She was a one-woman wrecking ball on a singular mission with nothing holding her back. She had known what she wanted to do since she was a little girl and was not shy in using her passion, personality, and a little bullying to get the job done. Although she spent her first decade cutting her teeth at smaller programs, in her mind, it was all a part of a larger journey that would one day take her to the heights of her profession.

Almost as if she was on a path parallel to Jo Ann's, Gloria Steinem was in the infancy of her career as a journalist and leader of the women's movement. With few if any role models in her career or ideology, Gloria was forced to chart her own pathway and to do so in a very public way. She cut her teeth in the South following the George

McGovern campaign and used her singular personality and her voice in the popular press to awaken a sleeping giant and establish a national movement. Gloria was more than capable, committed, and always willing to challenge the status quo. In this way, Gloria and Jo Ann were practically soul sisters.

After coming from a small rural school, Jo Ann landed at John Overton High School, where she thought she had died and gone to heaven. From her very first day she was a dominating force with ten years of teaching behind her and all of the opportunity in the world in front of her. She was experienced, confident, strong, and ready to make her mark on the world of music education. She had fought through inexperience and ignorance to establish herself and was ready to ascend to the next level. She had taught her students well and had become a better student herself. In her mind, each new day was an opportunity to change her students as well as change herself.

Jo Ann says she was a different person, and also notes that the students were different as well. In her early days, Overton was nicely nestled in the suburbs of Nashville, surrounded by sprawling estates belonging to country music stars and prominent politicians. Overton was as much a college preparatory school as it was a high school, and the students were engaged, educated, and reflective of their affluent community. But as is the case with all jewels, when overused and not maintained, they lose their sparkle.

After decades of use, John Overton High School has lost its sparkle. While the estate-like houses remain, the children who live in them no longer attend Overton. Once considered the crown jewel of the Nashville public school system, it is now showing its age and is fighting to stave off the effects of neglect and time. Where it once stood as a proud monument to public education, equal to all, Overton High School now pales in comparison to the opulent Franklin Road Academy, a private parochial school built directly adjacent to it. The students of the Awesome Overton Band, as they are known, are a more diverse group of students who face as many socioeconomic challenges as they do academic ones.

In her early years Jo Ann was more likely to ask what college you were going to rather than if you were going. In 1981 the Reagan administration was just getting up and running, and the K Car and the minivan were sweeping the country.

> Back when I first started teaching, it was more about me and what I was doing than the students. I was more focused on my success than theirs, but as the years passed, I began to figure things out. Once I saw that it wasn't about me, the program changed quickly and changed for the better. Building great performances started by building great kids and I believed that kids were kids... regardless of where you taught or where they lived. Once I realized that, we were able to build something special and to share it with our community. That was my focus when I got to Overton and has been ever since.

I think I have mellowed over the years, but my friends tell me that I'm full of crap. I do know that while my passion is the same, my delivery is different. Back then I wouldn't think twice about throwing a baton or yelling at a kid. Heck, you could kick a chair across the room and it was considered to be a display of discipline. I wouldn't do that now. I still get frustrated and yell, but in a very different way. In that way, I am a much better teacher now.

She pauses to think.

Back then, I never considered the ramifications of giving a kid a hug. I do now. I still hug 'em, but in the back of my mind, I worry about it. Things have changed a lot in my thirty-five years, myself included. In fact, I think it has been me who has changed the most.

Americans have a flair for the dramatic. We find the sixty-second sound bite and the emotional interview more interesting and engaging than the actual story or the information that surrounds it. Not having an important byline or eye-catching video doesn't make an event less newsworthy, just less interesting. Change is often marked and measured by traumatic events. We remember riots, walkouts, protests, and rallies, but real change often occurs in excruciatingly small increments in ways not covered by the evening news. People remember the historic vote on

Capital Hill for the Equal Rights Amendment, but real equality and real change was occurring daily in coffee shops, corporations, and classrooms.

In her three and a half decades, Jo Ann had thought she'd seen it all. Broken down buses, student walkouts, overprotective parents, and drug-sniffing dogs were just a sampling of her experiences. Through it all, she stood strong and resolute as a teacher and mentor to young people. You could disagree with her direction, but you had best keep it to yourself, because she was the captain of her ship. Even the smallest sign of mutiny meant that someone was going to walk the plank. Articulate, powerful, and in control at all times, she has been the real-life embodiment of the movement Gloria Steinem spoke so passionately about.

Few if any of the more than ten thousand students and parents Jo Ann has stood in front of can recall a time when she was at a loss for words. As public figures and sage speakers, people like Steinem and Hood are adept at speaking on the fly and waxing poetic in the moment. Jo Ann was not used to experiencing moments of unease or an inability to artfully share her message. She could not imagine a time when her professional vocabulary would prove to be inadequate for the job. As someone who had made her living by talking to young people, it seemed unlikely that after thirty five years her voice would leave her. Through it all—the death of a colleague, bomb threats, 9/11, natural disasters, and the unexpected passing of more than one student—she had something to say and a thought to share. But on October 27th, 2007, this all changed.

"Why now?" She wondered.

But her time for wondering was brief. 150 people were waiting for further instructions.

As Jo Ann takes a sip of her coffee, she recounts this day as if it were yesterday. She was in her thirty-fourth year of teaching and the twilight of her career. The end was in sight and retirement was imminent. Earlier in the day the band had performed at the Middle Tennessee State University, home of the venerable M.T.S.U. Contest of Champions, the longest running band competition in the United States. This was a place and an event she had known for the better part of forty years. In fact, she had been a part of this event since before her students and even some of their parents had existed. She competed in the contest when she was in high school, performed at it as a member of MTSU's Band of Blue, and had shared those same experiences with her students since 1972. Through it all, good times and bad times alike, she prepared bands and taught students what it meant to sacrifice in pursuit of excellence. In her years she had overcome bad drill, bad music, bad uniforms, bad choreography, better bands, and better teachers and always emerged as a champion. And in the state of Tennessee, that term is defined by the Contest of Champions. For nearly thirty-five years Jo Ann fought the good fight and never lost, until that day in 2007.

After receiving the results from the prelims, she paused to gather her thoughts. Realizing that the students were waiting for her, she knew her time for reflection was short.

The entire walk back to the busses through the parking lot adjacent to the stadium was spent plotting what she wanted to say. With every step she practiced it over and over in her mind, each time trying to find just the right words, just the right inflections, just the right facial expression to communicate her thoughts but not her emotions. She knew she had to say what needed to be said, but not share what she felt. So she practiced. But no matter how she phrased it, no matter the words she used, it still didn't feel right.

Jo Ann is someone who wears her heart on her sleeve and says what's on her mind. Filtering her words was not something she felt comfortable doing, and she knew that the kids would see through her facade. She knew that if she didn't phrase it just right, her students would know that they were being talked *at* and not talked *to*, and that was the last thing she wanted to do. After what seemed like the longest walk of her life, she gave up and decided that she would just speak from her heart.

When Jo Ann arrived at the band busses, the students were being fed and were beginning to sort through their equipment for the evening performance. This meal was the traditional precursor to the finals held later in the evening and was a time-honored tradition. Jo Ann says, "I watched kids being served by their parents, who twenty years earlier, were being fed by their own parents."

This meal was now bridging the gap between band generations that had never failed to make finals and had been perennial contenders for the top spot for a quarter of a century.

On this particular day, having drawn an early time slot for the prelims performance meant very little sleep for the students after a late arrival from an away game the night before. Band members, in the throes of a free-food frenzy, were socializing among themselves, and very few if any noticed her return to the site, much less the look of shock on her face. Besides, she always met with the staff before giving announcements and the schedule of events for their finals performance. It had been this way for twenty-seven years at John Overton High School. Why should it change now? Little did the students know, something very big was about to happen, as The Streak, as it's called in Tennessee, was coming to a close.

> I remember thinking how crazy this was. I knew that this day was coming, but after twenty-seven years, I didn't think it would be that day. I didn't know what to do or what to say. After so long, how could I have been so unprepared?

As dusk settled in and the warm sunlight gave way to a brisk chill, the students and staff gathered for their marching orders. As Jo Ann began to speak, she could feel her voice leaving her body. It was almost as if her vocal chords were paralyzed. She knew what she wanted to convey but was unable to say it.

"This is what it must be like to have a stroke," she thought.

After a lifetime as a public educator, after more than fifty thousand hours in front of young people, and after hundreds upon hundreds of experiences of speaking in public, her voice had left her. Not her ability to speak, but her voice. If you asked her what was the color of the sky or who she was going to vote for in the coming elections, she could have clearly articulated her thoughts; but her voice, the source of her ability to articulate the conscience and conviction of her soul, was gone. With each passing moment the silence grew more uncomfortable for students and staff alike. When it became almost unbearable, Jo Ann nodded to a parent who shared the news that there would be no more performances for the year. After twenty-six consecutive appearances as a finalist at the Contest of Champions, The Streak and their season was officially over.

> After the parent told them, several kids started to cry. They felt as if they had let us down, when in reality, I wondered if it was us that had let them down. Kids are kids... they were no different than the kids the year before that had been successful. What changed was not something in their control but within ours.

Music teachers often send mixed messages to their groups. They preach ownership and how the group is "your" group when in reality it isn't. Students don't create the show concept, arrange the music, or chart the drill. Students don't rehearse the band or choreograph the guard work; teachers do. The students may perform the show, but it is not *their* show. As directors it is hard but important to own up to our responsibilities in both successful and failed endeavors. Gloria Steinem states, "A pedestal is as much a prison as any small confined space." If we as teachers place ourselves on a pedestal, we must be prepared for the discomfort that can come with it. And Jo Ann Hood found out all about that feeling.

> I felt sick, not about the loss, but how the students felt. Through all of the emotion, I kept coming back to the thought that we were no longer a championship band. And I had to face the reality that it was possible that it was in part because I was no longer a championship teacher.
>
> As odd as it seems, as bad as I felt, there was almost a sense of relief. There were years that were close, and I knew that with the changing demographics of the school and cutbacks in the program that this was becoming less of a possibility and more of a reality. The hardest part for me was coming to grips with the fact that this might be more than a minor setback for the program. This could be our new reality. But for now, all I could do was focus on the here and now and the heartache that was written on the faces of those kids.

Over the years Jo Ann has learned that in order to be successful, the one constant is change. In order to be successful she had to accept and embrace the dynamic of change. Changing enrollment, demographics, values, and expectations, coupled with a dynamic and evolving art form meant that if she stood still for even a moment, she would be left behind.

> Teaching today is harder, no question. Kids today are different, but in many ways they're better. Believe it or not, in many ways, kids work harder today than ever before. Back when I started, we would rehearse maybe an hour a day, and our show had ten pages of drill... if that. Now kids are putting more time in on one Saturday than we used to do all week, and our most recent show had almost one hundred different sets. Back then, there is no way the kids would have rehearsed nearly as long or as hard as we do today.

> The demands we place on our students and ourselves today are much greater than twenty years ago, and through it all, they have risen to whatever was asked of them. And even today, my students not only work harder, they also play better. Much better. I go back and watch recordings of the bands during the glory years at Overton, when we won everything and had almost two hundred and fifty kids on the field.

The band didn't play nearly as well as they do now. I guess I am still amazed by the fact that a one hundred piece band of inner city kids in 2008 can out-play and out-march two hundred and fifty affluent suburbia kids from 1985.

People want to view the past through rose colored glasses, but in reality, what kids are being asked to achieve and the hours we are asking them to commit to were non-existent even fifteen years ago. Talent aside, kids are simply doing more and achieving more than ever before. If anything has changed, it is the teachers, not the kids. As we ask for greater accountability from the students, we must display greater accountability ourselves.

And there it is... the epiphany that defies, divides, and defines us as a profession. Yes, students are changing, but that does not necessarily mean for the worse. It is a time honored tradition for each generation to believe that their successors are somehow inferior to them. For hundreds of years people have bemoaned how their children and grandchildren have had it easier, all the while complaining that the world is getting more complex and harder to navigate.

Jo Ann knows that the key to her success is not in preparing her students but in preparing herself. She believes that equal to her instructional responsibilities is the responsibility to stay current and on the cutting edge. Throughout her career she joined every board imaginable, judged every show she was asked to, and served in every leadership role in the state. While others admired her service, few if any saw that her driving force was not just a desire to serve the profession but the desire to serve her band. In those roles she acquired tools and techniques that made her students and her ensembles successful. She knows that in front of great bands there are great teachers. Perhaps the reason she struggled so hard to tell her students that they were not champions was her startling realization that she was no longer a champion, either.

Like Gloria, Jo Ann possesses an acerbic wit and sharp tongue. She is known more for her fierce bark than her tame bite. Her face can display a range of emotions that most actors would envy, and she is not shy about using them. She is every bit as elegant as she is strong. Equally gruff and graceful, she is as comfortable hanging with the guys as she is chatting with her female cohorts. She can shoot the bull with the best of them, can tell a good joke, and is an accomplished bartender as much as she is a musician. She has no children but is fiercely maternal.

People who do not know her well often mistake her intensity and passion as a sign of someone who is brash and uncaring. But those who truly know her understand that she is emotional on a very deep level and that she cares very deeply for her students. Teaching is more than a job, it is a lifelong pursuit. She hides her emotions well, perhaps in part as a survival mechanism. Most see her persona but not the passion that drives it.

After spending decades in a male-dominated profession in which control and dominance were inexorably intertwined with excellence and success, she feels that she has little other choice. It worked well for her over the years, for by all accounts she is a highly successful woman that has been turning heads and taking names for longer than many of us have been alive. Through it all, as her environment has changed, so has she. In an almost chameleon-like way she has evolved and adapted with her professional environment.

When Jo Ann started teaching in 1972 there were little if any after-school marching rehearsals. All instruction took place during the school day. The marching band usually consisted of the school's top musicians and the auxiliary group consisted of two twirlers and the person who set their batons on fire. Bands typically attended only one or two festivals per year, and the show consisted of no more than twelve pages of drill. Students played grade-three music with flip folders. Concert band didn't start until November and jazz ensemble took place during the school day. There were few if any summer rehearsals, and music camps were month-long events designed for elite musicians and children of the affluent. Booster groups were minimal or nonexistent and there was almost no need to raise additional funds outside of what the school provided.

> Things were easier when I started. Back then, there were fewer distractions and opportunities for kids. After-school jobs were rare and easier,

as the kids were done with school by one o'clock. To be honest, when I started teaching, most kids only focused on school. As time passed, kids started taking on additional responsibilities and with the passage of Title 9, everything changed for girls. In my mind, that was what started the change in education. Now kids are spread more thinly and do more things for shorter periods of time. Kids today have developed a need for more instant gratification. They are raised in an environment where you have to teach them what a commitment is. Everything is so immediate in their world that you have to help them see the benefit of waiting and working for something. But then again, my parents said that about TV and my generation.

I do know that in the past thirty-five years my approach to teaching has changed. I try to give students a taste of success earlier in the rehearsal process to keep them coming back. And to keep them engaged, my rehearsals are faster paced and we cover more ground. I program differently now. I don't want to spend two months beating kids up to get them to learn something, so I am smarter about how I choose literature. I think the need to make my instruction more successful for kids and faster paced has made me a better teacher.

Another thing that has changed for teachers is the way we communicate and interact as colleagues. Even with all of the technology, we communicate less than ever on a meaningful level and almost never ask for help. Years ago we set our rehearsal and our personal schedules so that we could spend our "free" nights helping other groups rehearse. This never happens any more. We have become so tight lipped about things, like we are hiding state secrets or something. Our colleagues are our best and most underused resource and yet they are the people we call on the least.

As our memories fade, we often wax poetic about the good old days, sometimes forgetting the realties that came with it. Sure, things were simpler back in the day, but I for one have grown fond of modern conveniences like computerized drill charting, web pages, email, and Dr. Beat. It is important that, as we address the challenges associated with today's music education we also accept and celebrate our advances, both instructional and technological. Jo Ann thinks back to the realities of when she first stepped on a podium:

> When I started teaching, a director's desk drawer consisted of office supplies, grade books, charting paper, and was as likely to contain a bottle of scotch and a pack of cigarettes as a professional

trade journal and a tuning fork. Students were defiant and looking to vent their social angst on any authority figure that crossed their path. Sit-ins were common and the establishment was in the midst of turmoil. Facial hair and psychedelic drugs were in and winter guard and indoor drum line hadn't even been dreamed of. The days are the same length, and yet the to-do list outside of teaching continues to grow.

While most educators see the glass half empty, Jo Ann sees it as half full.

Teaching is easier now, with all of the resources we have. Instrument pedagogy has improved and we have greater access to tools and technology, both instructional and non-instructional. Computers have revolutionized just about everything we do and have made running the program infinitely easier. Despite all of this, a lot of young teachers just don't want to put in the time it takes to hone their craft and build a program.

I came out of college thinking I knew everything, but my first week of teaching quickly showed me that I knew nothing, and I went in search of those who did. It seems to me that young teachers today think they know more than they do and spend precious little time learning from those who do. I still pick up the phone constantly and call people for advice. I still go to clinics and learn from the best and I have been doing this a long time! I work more now than ever before and I am still learning something every single day. We seem to be looking for more to do instead of doing what we are doing better.

I love teaching now more than ever. I am better at it and I would never want to go back. These are the best days of my career. I could have retired years ago, but I just wasn't ready to leave. I still had more to learn and more to do, and besides, decline in enrollment and demographic changes had taken its toll on the once mighty Overton Band, and I was not about to leave until we had this thing turned around. So I am going to stay here until we can get this program back on the right track. People tell me I am crazy, but after so many wonderful years, I feel as if it's my responsibility to the program, the school, and most importantly, the students.

So instead of lamenting the kids of today, she and her co-director Debbie Burton dig their heels in and teach as hard as they ever have. As Jo Ann approaches the twilight of her career, she works even harder. She and Debbie go to more clinics, attend more conferences, and ask more questions than ever before. They understand not only the challenges in front of them but the teaching tools required to successfully overcome them.

> Kids today also face economic pressures to work, not to help their families, but to have things. I often ask kids why they work. They always say it's because they want a car. When I ask them why they need a car, they tell me it's so they can get to work. It seems like a vicious circle to me, but then I have to remember that we live in a different time, kids are different today, and that, I guess, has made me a better teacher. I teach more concepts now in a shorter period of time not because I want to, but because I have to.

Jo Ann understands the need to be an efficient and effective educator. She understands that the band is as much a reflection of her efforts as her students. A colleague of Jo Ann's and director at another preeminent program in the area said it best:

> Back then, just as today, if we got beat at a contest, it was by Jo Ann Hood. Not by her band, but by *her*. We had more staff, more students, and more talent. She just had more drive and out-taught us. How that woman has done what she has done for the past three and a half decades is beyond my comprehension. She is a force of nature. I am not

sure if it was part of her plan, or part of her nature, but she has seen it all, survived it all, and unlike most senior educators, is still standing among the top of the heap and leading the charge.

Educators are prone to espouse but not embrace change. Our professional landscape is littered aplenty with trends and techniques that were once hailed as revolutionary and are now laughed at as educational fads. Each and every day, schools around the country try to reinvent themselves so they can be perceived as modern and progressive. Our educational system is in perpetual pursuit of the singular idea which is sure to revolutionize teaching and learning. We look to experts and leaders to point us in the right direction and set us on the pathway. But great teachers have always understood that there is no silver bullet, no leader on a white horse, no one size that fits all solution. Almost as certainly as there are fifty million different students in the public schools of America, there are fifty million different ways to teach them. Given the complexities associated with providing instruction in varying areas each and every day, not including clubs and activities, the instructional possibilities balloon to an incomprehensible level. Add to this the day to day emotional, cognitive, and physiological changes that a teenager undergoes, and you can clearly see that a singular approach is a flawed one indeed. Yet despite institutional attempts for reformation, it is often the teachers themselves and not the students that fight back.

As music educators, we alone are responsible for increased standards of excellence. We alone are responsible for increased opportunities for student performance. We alone are responsible for the ever growing financial burdens that come with these standards and opportunities. We alone are responsible for the state of music education and are the sole stewards of its future. Given that, perhaps it is not students who are making teaching music more difficult, but teachers.

> If the shoe doesn't fit, must we change the foot?
> - *Gloria Steinem*

We are constantly evolving. With each passing day, change seems to come in larger quantities and at a faster rate than the day before. The same holds true for our profession. If you read a marching band adjudication rubric from 1972, it would pale in comparison to 2011. By 1980s standards, the achievement level of today seems unattainable. What drum corps were doing five years ago, high school groups are doing today; and what drum corps are doing in a stadium today will be the reality of a freshman's future. We have fundamentally changed not only our approach to the activity but the activity itself.

Change is almost a requisite for mere survival in our modern world. We crave the newest of everything: technology, fashion, information, location, etc.... How can we expect a teacher to not only last thirty years, but keep fresh, innovative, and excited about his job? And there stands the leader of the movement, the Gloria Steinem of music education: Ms. Jo Ann Hood.

Fast forward exactly twelve months from her darkest moment. Same Contest of Champions, different day.

> We had made finals. I cannot tell you what a relief it was. As much as we told the kids it didn't matter, it did, partly for them, partly for me. It was funny that after twenty-seven years of practicing for finals retreat, for the first time we didn't practice for Pass in Review. I wanted to, but Debbie didn't. We weren't even sure that year's show was better than last year's, so practicing for something that seemed unlikely was tempting fate.
>
> As they announced eighth place, we were relieved it wasn't us. Thankful that we had made finals, not being in last place seemed like an additional bonus. I knew we had a great show and I was just glad that I wasn't the only one who thought so. As they worked their way through seventh, sixth, fifth... we were still waiting to here our name. They had called out all of the past winners, and I began to believe. We had not won it since 1985 and I wasn't about to allow myself to believe in the possibility of us winning it again. After all, the bands that had already been called were almost twice the size

of us. They had experience, staff, and resources beyond anything we could match. They were programs of note and educators of substance.

As they announced third place, we knew we were down to the final two. The tension was palpable as the announcer milked every second to raise the audience to a fever pitch. I reached to Debbie and she screamed, "Leave me alone!" I screamed back "Too bad!" and grabbed her closer. The kids were frozen and took great pride in not moving, despite the two of us.

"In second place..." the announcer boomed...

And there it was. After twenty-three years, we had returned to the top. We had come from nowhere to first in twelve months. It was one of the happiest moments of my teaching career, not because of how we finished but how far we had come. I was happy for the school. I was happy for the parents, I was happy for the staff, and to be honest, I was happy for myself. Not because we had won, but because I knew that I still had the tools to teach. Most of all, I was happy for the kids. Most of these kids had not made finals, and the last time we won it, their parents were in band.

Jo Ann started teaching in 1972 hoping for moments like this. Thirty-five years later, she is living it, and through her tireless efforts to help her students grow, she is the one who how has grown the most. Her fear through it all had nothing to do with losing the contest; it had to do with losing her identity. For thirty-five years she has been a teacher, and a champion one at that.

> After the announcement, people flooded us with congratulatory hugs and well wishes. I could see that many of them were surprised with the results, but I wasn't. I knew how hard those kids had worked, and I knew how hard we had taught, and I knew that in combination, we could achieve anything. Debbie had designed the show from beginning to end. I was so proud of her. I was proud of our kids. I was proud to be a teacher of the Awesome Overton Band.

I have a feeling that if Gloria Steinem had been there... she would have been proud, too.

Chapter Nine

JUMPING OFF THE LADDER
On Professional Status in Music Education with Terry Jolley of Siegel Middle School

For Americans old enough to remember, the Iran hostage crisis was the singular defining moment in what can be described as America's darkest decade, the 1970s. A ten-year struggle with political corruption, double-digit inflation, a crippling energy crisis, high unemployment, and an unpopular war in Vietnam left the national ego bruised and confidence shaken. American morale was at an all time low and it seemed as if things couldn't get any worse. That is, until they did.

The harshest blow to the already fragile national psyche was struck on November 4, 1979, when Iranian militants took fifty-two United States Marines and embassy workers hostage in Tehran. The captors held the workers, and America's attention, hostage for four hundred forty-four days. The national nightmare got increasingly worse when, after failed attempts at negotiating a release, the U.S. military attempted a covert military rescue that was a spectacular failure of both planning and execution, and resulted in the deaths of eight Marines. The unfortunate and unnecessary loss of life and international embarrassment was an affront to what was long considered the world's best trained and equipped fighting force. More than anything, the international embarrassment fueled an already growing anti-American sentiment in the Middle East, and plummeted the United States into deeper despair.

With modern technology and extensive military training, it hardly seemed possible that the United States could be held hostage by a ragtag group of scantily armed, ill-trained, uneducated, religious fanatics. Americans were left to wonder, "If the elite soldiers of the special forces couldn't rescue the hostages, how could this possibly end well?"

The fourteen month nightmare came to a conclusion when the hostages were released at exactly twelve o'clock noon on January 20, 1981. While the secret negotiations were completed days in advance, the release was strategically timed to coincide with the swearing in of a new U.S. President. At exactly the same time that Ronald Reagan took the oath of office, fifty-three hostages walked free for the first time in fourteen months. Yes, I said fifty-three. While the fifty-two weary Americans were escorted out of the American embassy compound, the fifty-third and final hostage was escorted out of the Oval Office. James Earl Carter, the one term, thirty-ninth President of the United States was as much a hostage as those held captive in the American embassy. They were hostages of the same cause, in two very different locations. Few remember and even fewer history books mention that, as a show of support and personal resolve, President Carter pledged to not leave the White House to campaign for reelection until the hostages were freed, virtually guaranteeing the end to his presidency.

As a person and President, Jimmy Carter is the very embodiment of the American dream. His life story reads as much like a fairy tale or an American propaganda pamphlet as it does a biography. Raised in poverty in Plains, Georgia, he used his people skills, work ethic and ingenuity to rise to the highest office in the land.

Born from two working class parents on October 1, 1924, James Earl Carter, better known as "Jimmy," gave no early indication of his leadership prowess. Few who knew him as a child thought him to be anything other than normal. Early on, he gave no indication that he would be the head of anything other than his father's peanut farm, much less the head of state. A born again Christian known for his love of blue jeans and all things Bob Dylan, Jimmy's plainspoken style and folksy approach endeared him to his constituents and his country. In a time where political distrust was at an all-time high, Jimmy Carter was the antidote to what ailed the country. He was an honest man who worked tirelessly to restore integrity to America's highest office and trust among its citizenry.

Carter followed a traditional path out of his rural surroundings: good grades, hard work and the desire to be a part of something bigger than his small home town of four hundred people. He attended a local community college and Georgia State University, where he pursued mathematics and then qualified for the United States Naval Academy. After graduating from the Academy near the top of his class, he successfully served in a variety of roles throughout the Navy's above water fleet. He was viewed by many as a rising star and future ship commander, until he made the decision to step back and apply to the submariner program. Some saw his return to school and a new class of service as a career threatening move, but not Jimmy. He believed that the broader his base of knowledge and skills, the faster he could climb.

It didn't take long for Carter to get noticed in his new surroundings. He was a standout among his peers and classmates and he soon caught the eye of Admiral Adam Rickover. Rickover saw Carter's intellect and leadership skills as strong assets and had him transferred to the nation's newest secret project, the Navy's fledgling nuclear submarine program. As a part of his new assignment, Jimmy studied and was trained in the evolving field of nuclear physics. After completing his training, he returned to active duty and was back on the fast-track to success. He was commissioned as an officer aboard the nation's first nuclear submarine, the Nautilus. Jimmy Carter was among the Navy's brightest young stars. Until he walked away from it all.

In the spring of 1953, Jimmy received the news that his father had died. The unexpected passing shook him to the core and made him reevaluate his priorities in life. After much prayer and consultation with his wife Roselynn, he decided to leave the Navy and return to civilian life to care for his mother and run the family's peanut farm. In that instant, he became quite possibly the most highly educated and expensively trained peanut farmer in the world.

Jimmy made the adjustment back to rural life and settled in with his wife and three children for the long and difficult life of a farmer. By all accounts he was a model citizen and family man. He went to church, taught Sunday school, and made it a point to reach out to fellow neighbors and people in need. In this way and many others, James Earl Carter was just like everyone else, except for one small thing. He was happy, but not completely content.

While married life and quiet living as a farmer suited Jimmy's personality, his personal faith and sense of community left him with a yearning to make a difference for those around him. He felt an inner drive to do something more. In an attempt fill that void, Jimmy ran for and won a vacant seat in the Georgia State Legislature. To the political experts, it seemed improbable that someone with no experience, from a town lacking the presence of a large voting block could get elected in his first attempt at public office. However, Jimmy Carter was the poster child for improbable. Even as a political novice, his earnest desire to use power for good resonated with his constituents. Jimmy didn't see the office as a stepping stone to another office, but as an opportunity to serve his neighbors and fellow Georgians. He saw it as a way to make a difference. No one, least of all Carter, could have seen that his future would take him from the Georgia State House, to the Governor's mansion and on to the Oval Office. Jimmy Carter was living proof that with hard work and desire, a person could become anything, even President of the United States.

* * *

Beyond the obvious personal charisma and southern charm, Terry Jolley and our thirty-ninth President share more than one might think. While no one would ever confuse Carter's slight frame and thick hair with Terry's imposing frame and ever-thinning hair, there is more similarity than meets the eye. I believe that if you were to spend five minutes with either one of them, you would know how truly similar they are. Both were born to working-class parents who placed a premium on civility and hard work. Although their upbringing was separated by forty years and four hundred miles, you can't help but wonder if, given the opportunity to meet, they wouldn't become fast friends. Politics aside, I could easily see the two of them, sitting on the front porch, swapping stories over a glass of sweet tea. They did meet once, although the separation in age and communication gap proved to be too much of an obstacle for any real communication. Terry says,

> I met Jimmy Carter when I was two years old, but of course – I don't remember that. In fact, I don't remember much from his Presidency at all. I was pretty young during his term of office. I do remember my dad talking about him and

I remember thinking it was cool that he had a kid my age and that she was famous. My dad worked hard at making sure we understood that the world outside our little town was full of amazing people doing amazing things.

Terry Jolley was raised in the small town of Dercherd, Tennessee. From the beginning, he and his sister were immersed in the world of music and it soon became evident that he was destined to follow in the footsteps of his mother, an elementary music teacher. Terry played in the band and the church where his father was the congregation's music minister and his mother, the pianist. Nurture versus nature arguments aside, Terry's talent and musical upbringing made music education seem like an easy and obvious choice. Like most music majors, he dreamed of one day standing in front of a fine ensemble, creating soaring melodies, and helping young people reach their true and full potential. Like many young teachers, he learned that his dream would have to start in a different place, teaching very different things.

In 1992, with a down economy and few teaching opportunities, Terry accepted the music teacher position at Warren County High School. Teaching sixth through twelfth grade band and choir meant that the soaring melodies he once dreamed of would have to wait until he taught them how to put their instruments together and empty the spit valves. At least he knew how to do that. Teaching choir would be another story all together. Until now, Terry's only experience in singing was in music theory and his voice was anything but operatic. Though he was trained for more, this was his only opportunity. He had found the musical equivalent of peanut farming, and was happy to be there.

Like Carter, Terry was happy in his initial surroundings, but not content. After two years in the job, he found himself making the jump to an assistant position in a large and very prestigious program. Terry spent four years cutting his educational teeth and developing a reputation as someone with musical chops, a good ear, and strong classroom management skills. He was happy to be an assistant; it provided him with greater opportunities on the podium, and the chance to work side-by-side with a master teacher. Terry was on his way up and climbing at a brisk pace. Everyone who watched him work knew that he was not long for the high school band room and would soon be standing at the top of the profession in the college or professional conducting ranks.

When asked about Terry, his mentor and friend said, "He was amazing! He was an old soul in a young body. Way wiser than his years. He was a joy and lots of fun to work with. The kids loved him and he loved them."

I asked Terry about his experiences as an assistant. He said,

> I learned a lot in those four years, not just about how to teach, but about myself. For the first time, I was a part of a "winning" program, and I was faced with the challenge of learning how

to balance competition with education. I had to decide what I *really* wanted to teach kids about music. I learned about what really mattered in life. I also learned that I *hated* lunch duty. The best part was that through it all, I was fortunate to be mentored by a veteran teacher. I knew that I had made the right decision and that it was a step up personally and professionally.

It is the last sentence that resonates. Did he receive more money at this new school? No. Did he have more student contact? No. Was there greater prestige in working for someone else? No. Why did he consider this move to be a step up? In another setting, the move he made would be seen as a lateral move at best. But band director and banker are two very different professions.

Climbing the professional ladder is as much a part of the American identity as apple pie and baseball. From a very young age we are taught that with hard work and determination, anything is possible and the sky is the limit. The "the sky is the limit" message can be inspiring and empowering. However, the covert subtext implies that if you fail to achieve success, it is due to your own inadequacy. While success is measured differently in the field of education, the ladder of success is just as present. In business, it is measured through advanced job titles and six figure salaries. In education, through advanced degrees and the opportunity to teach more skilled students. Regardless of the yardstick, the objective is the same; and hard work and perseverance will afford you advanced opportunities and greater rewards.

In business and education, the ladder of success is equally embedded but approached very differently. There is a definitive hierarchy and professional status that is associated with the various levels of teaching music. It isn't written down anywhere or taught in college practicum, but it exists. At the heart of this ill-defined hierarchy are two core beliefs. First, the better the ensemble, the better the job. Second, more advanced performers require more advanced teachers. While there is some merit and logic to this thought process, it is far from absolute and even further from reality. The blanket and perhaps natural assumption that the best teachers will advance to work with the best ensembles is based on the somewhat false precept that great ensembles are solely the result of great teaching. Of course the quality of the ensemble directly correlates to the quality of the teaching, but does this mean that there are no great beginning band teachers? Does this mean that beginning band should be taught only by beginning teachers? Don't we agree that elementary teachers require a greater understanding of instrument pedagogy? Is there not merit to placing our best teachers with our youngest students in the hope of building a strong musical foundation? Would we have successful high school bands without successful elementary music teachers? Should *Go Tell Aunt Rhodie* and *Begin the Beguine* have equal stature in our profession to the *Holst's Suite in Eb*? Is our ladder of success in music education based on *music* or *education*? The answer to this question is key to understanding how we view and quantify success. Success based solely in music would dictate that higher level performing ensembles are the pinnacle that we all aspire for. Success based solely in education would place the greatest importance on the foundation laid in the elementary setting. It is when the two evaluators are combined into one job title, music educator, we have a job description that lacks clarity. I asked Terry about this,

> I am challenged as an educator more in my junior high classroom than I ever was in the collegiate setting. It's not like classroom management or pedagogy was an issue with twenty-year old students who were studying privately. However, as a musician, I miss the musical setting of a university podium. I have enjoyed the challenges of both worlds, but for very different reasons.

If anyone has an understanding of the difference between *music education* and *educational music*, it's Terry Jolley. He has been up and down that ladder more than anyone I know.

During his fourth year as an assistant high school director, Terry was recruited to become the Associate Director of Bands at Middle Tennessee State University. This once proud program had fallen on hard times and was in need of someone who could provide the high energy and intense atmosphere that college students crave. While at the university, Terry also took the helm of the Middle Tennessee

Valley Winds, an ensemble of semiprofessional wind players that had recently played at the *Midwest Clinic*. When I asked about his desire to keep moving up he responded,

> I would say that my decisions to move, not just in moving to college but moving to a bigger high school program, were based on the possibilities of higher level literature. I truly enjoyed working with the college musicians; we could work fast and put some nice things together quickly. As you know, that doesn't happen in a middle school setting. The musical payoff is totally different. As I get older and more experienced, I have learned to enjoy the students' musical conquests on their level and try not to pay as much attention to my own personal musical desires.

Terry spent four successful years at MTSU and built the *Band of Blue* from sixty to over three hundred students. The transformation in his ensembles was dramatic and impressive. If you had asked any of his professional colleagues they would have said that Terry had risen to the top and was enjoying every minute. But if you had asked Terry, he would have told you a different story.

Terry Jolley had become the Jimmy Carter of our profession. He was the musical equivalent of the peanut farmer who rose to the Oval Office. In six short years, this small town boy rocketed through the ranks from beginning band to big time college band. He was the envy of many and enjoyed what he did. He was at the pinnacle of the profession, but as time passed, he began to feel that his off-podium responsibilities were demanding too much of his time. With each passing semester, it seemed as if his contact time with students was being replaced with more meetings and even more responsibilities that had nothing to do with teaching and learning. He was spending more time in front of a computer and less time in front of students. He remembers feeling frustrated and increasingly isolated, until one day, he realized that he had been taken hostage in his very own office. It seemed like he never left and that no matter what he did, he could not break free of its increasing hold on him. He knew something had to change, while everyone was looking up to him, he found himself looking to make a change. He remembers the day he came to that realization like it was yesterday.

> I have always had an open door policy so students could stop by and chat about school, life, music, or whatever. On one particularly busy day, a student stopped by and asked to chat. I told him I was too busy right now, but he could come back tomorrow. About thirty minutes later, it hit me that the reason I wanted to teach was to be there for the *students*. As soon as I realized it, I called that young man and asked him to meet me for dinner. When I got home that night, I spoke with my wife Alison about making a change.

Most young music educators dream of standing in front of skilled ensembles and running large programs. Why? Advanced programs require more work. Advanced programs typically comes with greater public scrutiny and higher expectations. Advanced programs need more management, oversight, and involvement. In business, greater work and responsibility yield greater financial gain, but that doesn't hold true in music. Small stipends associated with teaching at the secondary level pale in comparison to increased demand and rarely amount to more than a minimum wage per hour stipend for a maximum pressure job. To shatter another myth: collegiate positions usually pay even less than the public school sector does. Terry says,

> That's the greatest misconception about teaching college. Everyone thinks that the money and the perks are better and it just isn't true. The money (both personal and budgetary) are very limited at the university level. If you were to compare my budget and responsibilities as a high school teacher to that of a college director, I had more responsibility and was making less money at M.T.S.U than I did in the public schools.

This performance oriented hierarchy is based on musical demand more so than educational pedagogy. From the very first playing test in elementary school, students are taught to strive for better chair placement and more advanced ensembles. The commonly held belief is that more difficult literature presents greater learning opportunities and that more notes mean more challenging music. Conductors treat sheet music and score study as a musical Rorscach test (inkblot on white paper). When conductors study scores filled with technical passages and fast tempos they see musical prestige and power. As time passes and young teachers progress through their musical training, this belief system is reinforced. We have made the decision that we are music educators and not educators of music. As a profession, we have decided to use music as our carrot and our measuring stick.

Assuming you agree, let me ask you a few questions. Why do you want to conduct the top band more than the beginning band? Do prefer to rehearse technique to tone? Do you take more pride in advanced students or beginning ones? Is this a conscious choice you have made that meets with your educational philosophy or are you just responding to the musical bell like Pavlov's dog?

The value system that associates the skill sets of the students with those of the conductor is deeply flawed and embedded not just among teachers but parents as well. A former student and current colleague who has taught in both the junior high and senior high settings shared this with me.

"You have no idea how many times parents would say things like, 'You are doing such a good job and soon you will be teaching high school.' Or, 'Don't you wish you could be working with high school kids?' It was maddening. They might as well have said, 'Your job isn't good enough and if you don't advance, neither are you.' It never dawned on them that I was where I wanted to be and doing what I wanted to be doing. They assumed that if I stayed at the elementary level, it was because I wasn't good enough to teach high school."

There is no question that a career ladder exists in music education. You won't find it written about in a textbook or in any music education philosophy statements. When asked about philosophy, most professionals would say that the foundation of music education is established in the primary grades. They will speak passionately about investing in general music and the need for master teachers to return to the elementary classrooms of America. However, when asked where they want to teach, the answer is usually advanced education. This is where NIMBY (not in my back yard) comes into play. Everyone knows that it's important, but most of us think that someone else should be doing it.

As Terry points out, accepting less money for greater responsibility is an established part of our professional landscape and in this, we are not alone. The culture of education as a whole operates under a different value system that that of the business world. Teachers understand and often expect low wages and a lack of advancement opportunities as a tradeoff for pursuing the passion to teach. In recent years, politicians and educational reformers have tried a performance based incentive system to no avail. The practice of tying teacher pay to student performance on standardized tests rails against the very reason most teachers enter the profession: the desire to help young people to be successful. To use money to motivate someone who chose a profession in spite of low pay is misguided at best. If we are to attract and retain more successful teachers, an incentivized system based on intrinsic rewards needs to be developed and implemented. This is not to say that most teachers would not appreciate a larger salary, but it is not paramount in the hierarchy of professional rewards. As evidence of that, a recent study by the Morrison Institute of Public Policy polled a large sampling of educators and found that increasing financial gain did not make the top five indicators for increasing job satisfaction among public school teachers.

In the 2010 landmark book, *DRIVE: The Surprising Truth About What Motivates Us*, author Daniel Pink studied human motivation and its effects on job performance and satisfaction. His results were striking and stand in stark contrast to the way that corporate America has been operating for decades. Through his research, Pink discovered that an employee's belief that his work served a greater moral purpose or provided a communal benefit had the most significant impact on job performance and satisfaction. He surmised that workers work best when motivated by altruism, not financial gain. When he examined the world of education, he found that the same held true among teachers.

The first comprehensive study of this approach, from the Nashville Public Schools, showed the effect of merit based pay to be virtually nonexistent. The students of incentivized teachers did no better than the students of teachers paid regular salaries.

Since then, an even bigger study has come from Roland Fryer, a prominent Harvard economist who was originally an advocate for incentivized pay for educators. In his work, he examined the effects of pay-for-performance in the New York City Public Schools and found no evidence that teacher incentives increased student performance, attendance, or graduation. Nor did he find any evidence that the incentives changed student or teacher behavior. If anything, teacher incentives may have decreased student achievement, especially in larger schools.

Most music educators view aesthetic opportunity, the ability to create and conduct music at a very high level at the very heart of their professional reward system. This is why Terry's decision to leave M.T.S.U. was puzzling to his friends and colleagues. To their way of thinking, he was at the top and looking down on the rest of the world; the quality and growth of the bands at M.T.S.U had been nothing short of extraordinary. Those who didn't know him well would never have guessed that after six amazing years, Terry had grown to see his office as a prison. While he enjoyed his fellow educators and students, he knew that once paroled, he would not likely return.

> As soon as I started looking, people started asking why. They couldn't understand why I would leave such a great job. Honestly, there were moments I agreed, but I knew that it was the wrong place for me.

> It was a very difficult process, deciding what to do next. I didn't know where to go or what to do. The decision to leave was a difficult one as there are very few people I could call for advice. I mean, how many people do you know that walked away from a college job at the age of thirty-six? Normally, at this age, most directors would be looking for the next rung up, or better job, but I didn't want to climb the ladder, I wanted to jump off of it!

Terry made the decision to take his years of experience and countless connections as a music educator and start his own company, *Jolley and Associates*. His dream was to provide educational and professional resources to music educators from all levels and all areas. He took his arranging skills, his experience as a teacher, and his innate people skills to help others succeed. He began to write, arrange, judge, clinic, guest conduct, evaluate, and do whatever else was necessary to see more teachers succeed.

> It was scary. I didn't know if or how successful the business would be. What I came to realize was that running a business requires a different type of organizational thought, but a thought process not all that different from being a band director. You work with a variety of people in search of solutions. It's similar to handling your booster club, but you're not dealing with volunteers, so

you're responsible for the hiring and firing of everyone involved.

I loved working for myself. It was great being able to set my own schedule or go watch someone teach any time I wanted to. It was also great to have the freedom to spend time on some personal aspects of life. I was the most healthy during this period. But things change.

The change Terry mentions was the birth of his daughter Ava. With her, everything changed... personally *and* professionally.

My wife Alison, who was a nurse, wanted to spend some time at home with Ava which required us to make some adjustments. The financial demands of adding a child to this world, plus giving Alison the time she wanted, made the financial irregularities of self employment more difficult to bear.

Now, just as his business was beginning to grow, Terry made the decision to climb back down the ladder. He knew that he could not and would not return to the collegiate setting, so he looked elsewhere. Terry returned to the public school system and joined the staff at Blackman High School. The idea of a hugely successful collegiate marching band director teaching music for a school whose marching band didn't even participate in competition was puzzling to many, but not to Terry.

> I loved working at Blackman. I was working with someone I trusted in a setting that was unique. We didn't do the competitive marching band scene, which was a change for me, but a good one. We had a marching band of almost two hundred kids that was fronted by a rock band. I arranged all the charts and had a blast doing it. The marching band rehearsed one night a week and let me tell you, cleaning drill was not a high priority for us; giving the kids a good experience was.
>
> This was the most musical group of students I had ever worked with. Conducting this group was like being in front of an honor band every day.

Again, Terry was faced with his old nemesis, lunch room duty and bus rides. You would think that the return to the classroom after a successful career as a collegiate director and business owner would fracture the ego, but not for Terry.

> I don't think I ever consciously thought about "the ladder." I do remember wondering if it was the right thing to do, but I guess each job served its purpose and taught me something different

about teaching and myself. While it's true that there are musical limitations at each level, I have come to understand that students will always rise to the occasion.

Terry spent two years at Blackman before change came again. His best friend, Phillip Gregory, had an opening for an assistant at his middle school (Seigel) and asked Terry to join him there. It had been almost fifteen years since Terry started his career teaching middle school and he was concerned that after being so far removed from that setting, he might not be successful or even happy teaching at this level. But the opportunity to spend his days with his best friend was too much to pass up.

The desire to better ourselves is not limited to the field of education. Wherever you look in life you will find many examples of ordinary people doing extraordinary things. What makes music educators different from our nonmusical peers is not that we desire success, but how we define it. Different professions place value and importance on different things. The business world typically places more value on where they work rather than the work they do. In this value system, one's job title and position is more than a business card, it is a statement of importance and level of accomplishment. Music education not much different, except for the people at the bottom, general music teachers, rarely have business cards to hand out. This is antithetical to the belief that a strong foundation is required for any person or any ensemble to be successful. If this were the case, successful general music teachers would be the CEO's of our industry and commonly recognized names within our professional ranks.

For high school and collegiate conductors, success is highly dependent on the people who trained the students before them. The general music teacher creates interest, the elementary teacher establishes the fundamentals, and the middle school teacher shapes the concept of ensemble behaviors that lead to musical success. This hierarchy places elementary general music teachers at the top of the chain of command in music education. Without the elementary music teachers, high school directors would be waving their beautiful mahogany Mollard batons to an empty room.

> I thought I knew how music education worked, but I didn't truly understand it until I got to Siegle Middle School. There, I got the chance to reunite with a former student, Alexis Derryberry, who was the school's general music teacher and musical pied piper. Watching her teach was like watching a great conductor on a podium. She was able to bring things out of her students that I didn't even know were there. For the first time, I got to witness a truly gifted teacher working not with a baton, but with Orff instruments and rhythm sticks. I was able to see the impact general music had not only on the success of the band program, but the success of every student she taught.

As someone who has spent a fair amount of time climbing and down the ladder, I asked Terry if he viewed the climb differently now than he did when he first started.

> I think that you have to be happy with yourself first, then be happy with your decision to "be where you are." This way, you don't spend so much time looking at your neighbor's grass as you do cutting your own yard.
>
> A job is what you make it, so don't spend your time thinking about the things you don't get to do instead of the opportunities in front of you. Whether you aspire for more musical responsibility or less, the education part doesn't change. You have to be happy as a teacher first and a musician second.
>
> We all handle things so differently that it's important to consider your personality when changing jobs. If literature is important to you, great; just know that middle school might not be where you will feel best. If you enjoy working with parents and doing the "Saturday Shuffle," then high school is probably a place where you will be happy. Sometimes people promote themselves to the level of their own unhappiness.

On January 20, 1981, the thirty-ninth President of the United States was released to begin the rest of his life. Carter was an iconic if not occasionally comic figure whose accomplished and turbulent Presidency was as volatile as it was significant. His presidential tenure included brokering a major Middle East peace accord, a weapons treaty with the Soviet Union, establishment of diplomatic relations with China, two new cabinet level departments, and the creation of the first comprehensive national energy plan. In addition, he guided the country through two national disasters, the eruption at Mount St. Helens and the Three-Mile Island nuclear disaster. Regardless of their political views, most presidential historians agree that Carter's single term as President of the United States was one of the most active in modern history. And yet, it is the post-presidency of Jimmy Carter that has provided the most insight to who he is as a person.

Most people consider Jimmy Carter to be the nation's greatest former President. He became a champion of human rights and founded the Carter Presidential Center, an internationally recognized organization for the protection of human rights. Additionally, Carter has been a tireless worker and visible participant for Habitat for Humanity International, an organization that works worldwide to provide housing for those in need. To this day, Jimmy Carter is the only President of the United States to win a Nobel Prize after leaving office and stands as one of the true international giants in the area of human rights. Time Magazine states, "While other former presidents played golf or made speeches, Carter, like some jazzed superhero, circles the globe at 30,000 feet, seeking opportunities to do good."

> I can't deny I'm a better ex-president than I was a president!
> President Carter
> *Washington Times (November 3, 2005)*

At the printing of this book, Terry Jolley has finished his downward climb and is preparing to leave the music world. His success as an educator afforded him the opportunity to return to his roots as an elementary educator, this time working with students from the entire county.

As music educators, we are always looking to climb the ladder of success. Higher ratings, better ensembles, larger audiences and more challenging literature are some of the rungs we aspire to reach. We do this for the good of our students, sometimes failing to remember that the ladder goes both up and down and can leave us stuck in a place where we are unhappy and alone.

Jimmy Carter, a nuclear scientist and former leader of the free world knew freedom when he saw it at the bottom of the ladder.

> Someone once said, and I agree with them, that Jimmy Carter is the only man in American history who used the United States presidency as a stepping stone to greatness.
> Jack Watson
> *Former White House Aide*

Terry Jolley is the only man I know who used his position as a college band director as a stepping stone to become a true educator. He would be the first one to tell you that, but he can't, he has lunch duty.

About the Author

For almost a decade Scott has been educating and entertaining student and adult audiences of all ages through his workshops and keynote presentations. Comfortable in large and small venues alike, Scott consistently finds creative ways to ensure laughter in learning as he provides for attendees the tools necessary to deal with their own lives, their organizations, and their schools. He not only provides an insightful educational presentation, but also provides his audiences direction on how to implement their newfound knowledge in action. Scott's workshops are a perfect companion to his keynote presentations and can be customized and/or created to meet your organization's needs.

Scott is the author of *Leadership Travel Guide*, a 240-page interactive leadership workbook. In addition he has two instructional videos, *Leadership Success* and *Leadership Survival Guide*, both of which are accompanied by a CD-ROM with downloadable curricula.

Mr. Lang currently resides in Chandler, Arizona with his beautiful wife, Leah, and their two children, Brayden and Evan. He can often be found at home changing diapers and sweeping up the tremendous amount of dog hair their Golden Retriever Rexi leaves behind.

Booking Scott

Scott Lang is a nationally renowned authority in the development of student leadership. His unique blend of candor, humor, and energy will challenge and move your group members to action as they strive for greatness in their personal and academic endeavors.

More than a workshop, it's a daily decision! Let Scott join your group's journey in creating a culture of success through one of his powerful workshop or presentations.

Scott can be reached via the web at www.scottlang.net or emailed at scott@scottlang.net.